John Roach

WHILE I HAVE YOUR ATTENTION

LITTLE CREEK PRESS®
AND BOOK DESIGN
Mineral Point, Wisconsin USA

T0108055

Little Creek Press® and Book Design
A Division of Kristin Mitchell Design, Inc
Mineral Point, Wisconsin
www.littlecreekpress.com

First Edition October 2018

For more information or to order books:
www.littlecreekpress.com

Printed in the United States of America

Library of Congress Control Number: 2018957005

ISBN-10: 1-942586-44-2
ISBN-13: 978-1-942586-44-9

To my parents, John and Mary Gene.

TABLE OF CONTENTS

◤ FOREWORD

Writers are like neurotic cats you cannot herd but must somehow move in the same general direction, which in my case was the printed page of *Madison Magazine*, where I served as an editor for 15 years.

If you know John Roach even a little, you know that he does not care to be herded in any direction that is not of his own volition. He is Irish; therefore, he is hard-headed. Which is why the back page of a magazine was—and is—the singularly best position for his column, originally called "Out There" when my predecessor Doug Moe introduced the column in 1993. You never, ever knew where John was headed, and that was half the fun of it. The other half was his uncommon way with words.

I had a litmus test for the quality of John's columns. They were at their best when I had wiped away a tear, felt a butterfly in my stomach, winced, or laughed out loud by the time I'd read the last word. Of course, there was the occasional phone call to John after I finished reading a particularly, shall we say, opinionated piece that challenged a specific person, place, thing, or idea.

"Do you really want to say that?" I'd ask. "Yes," he'd answer, followed by an oral argument that I almost never won.

An editor's job is hard. Damn hard. It also is incredibly rewarding. You get to coach, counsel, teach, learn and grow with some of the smartest, funniest, and most passionate people on the planet. John is all of those and then some. I'd add big-hearted, even though he may be loathe to admit it.

I once asked John how he comes up with his column ideas. "Easy," he said. "You wet your finger and put it in the air to see which way the wind is blowing." Fortunately for the readers of *Madison Magazine*, the wind is rarely calm.

After 25 years, John Roach has become as indigenous to Wisconsin as badgers and brats; to Madison as State Street and Vilas Park; and to the North Woods as lake sunsets and the call of the loon. Being John's editor, then and now for this latest compilation of his greatest hits, has been a privilege, a pleasure, and always an adventure.

~Brennan Nardi

◤ PROLOGUE

There are three people who played a critical role in this compilation of the last fifteen years of my 25-year run at *Madison Magazine*. First, Doug Moe, who in 1993 dared me to write a column. Mike Kornemann, who was a constant supporter of the column. And most importantly, Brennan Nardi, my former boss at the magazine and editor of this book. Brennan has perfected the art of being charming while telling me exactly what to do. The best compliment a writer can pay to an editor is that you trust them. I trust Brennan.

Also grateful for my current cohorts at the magazine, Andrea Behling and Karen Lincoln Michel.

I've learned things writing this column. First, it's a wonderful thing to have a platform to hold forth about the town, state, and friends you have known for 65 years. It's also a good thing for a human to be forced to sit down and ponder, at least once a month, what is important, powerful, or funny in the world. And then write about it. There is also something to be said for doing a job as best you can for twenty-five years in a row. I've never viewed myself as particularly dogged, but this column is the exception.

Finally, thanks to my family; Diane, Katie, Maggie, and JT, who tolerate and inspire me. They are the best thing in my life.

Nothing else compares.

TAKE A KNEE

Some of those with a flag on their jacket also think they are
uniquely qualified to determine who else is a patriot and who isn't,
ignorant of the fact that some of the least patriotic citizens in
our history have wrapped themselves in the flag
while walking all over our Constitution.

06.08
DEATH BY LAUGHTER

We embrace as well as any other tribe mankind's eternal desire to alter consciousness for distraction and solace from life's banality and pain.

We embrace as well as any other tribe mankind's eternal desire to alter consciousness for distraction and solace from life's banality and pain.

Tommy Farley sent along an advanced copy of the book he co-authored, along with the talented Tanner Colby, about his brother Chris.

It is a good read.

But the show biz triumphs and travails of Madison's comedic son were of less interest to me than the spot-on snapshot of the life the Farley family lived in Madison and the role that alcohol played in that existence.

It was less a condemnation of the lifestyle than an honest assessment. An assessment that could be made of many Madison and Wisconsin families. Including mine.

The Chris Farley Show speaks of the link between social, hale-fellow-well-met drinking and the slide that happens when that consumption becomes personally destructive, as it did in the case of young Chris.

As a Madison Irish, I can attest to the siren song of beers at the rail with friends. It is the life that I grew up with. And much of it is good. Some of the best times I have ever had have been over foaming heads when the singing starts.

But for me, and many others, it is a dangerous dance.

The truth is that we drink a lot in Wisconsin. What's more, we are proud of it. And if you are Irish, double it. We embrace as well as any other tribe mankind's eternal desire to alter consciousness for distraction and solace from life's banality and pain. It makes us colorful and fun on the stool, but behind the mirth there is sadness and regret.

We all know the friends who are haunted by their consumption. As we know and admire the brave ones who finally confronted the fact that they could no longer drink and stopped.

What made the Farley book so powerful for me is that I know many of the young men quoted in the book. They are members of my younger brothers' posse, and so they are members of mine. I have been golfing, fishing and sipping with all of them.

It is important to note that although Chris Farley was funny, he was not the only guy in that Madison gang who could make you laugh. They all could … and still can.

In fact, I can say without any hesitation that they are the funniest squad of guys you could ever share a beer with. They possess a collective comedic gift created by a strange blend of Madison ethnicity, family, time and locale that is truly rare. But that collective gift is also a curse. A curse that killed Chris Farley.

What the book so poignantly details is the burden of the funny drinker. Of how every bar becomes a stage. And every show requires Herculean consumption. Chris felt that burden, and according to those closest to him, would have fallen under that weight regardless of fame.

Since Chris' death his brother Tommy has attempted to make some sense of it. To do the Catholic thing and help others learn from the tragedy. All Tom really has to do is have folks read the book.

It will help us understand the brutal truth of excess and humor.

Of the laughs and madness at midnight and the unbearable sorrow of morning.

It is the awful truth of the funny drunk.

If you are sad, generous, haunted and gifted enough, folks will let you die alone for their amusement.

05.10
MADISON AND THE POPE

Murphy's case is the gun that won't stop smoking.

One of the guys from the old neighborhood made *The New York Times* in March. Wish it were under better circumstances.

Steve Geier grew up a Madison west-sider, just off Monroe Street on Terry Place along the shores of Lake Wingra. He was, and is, part of a big

Geier clan in Madison. Steve lost his hearing after a bout of rheumatic fever when young.

Those of us who knew Steve understood that he was deaf. We also knew he wasn't dumb. He was, and is, a smart, tough, likable cat. Like many of the Geiers, he was a fine athlete. Steve in particular was strong like an ox. As my brother Bob reminded me, Steve would regularly jack a misplaced pitch into Lake Wingra from the ball diamond back by the boathouse.

Steve made *The New York Times* with an excerpted interview conducted by former *Capital Times* reporter David Callender. In the interview Steve, for the first time in public, detailed in graphic terms how, at the age of fourteen, he was raped by Father Lawrence C. Murphy. Tough story for a 60-year-old married dad to tell to all.

Tougher yet, Steve was one of nearly 200 deaf boys raped and abused by Murphy at the St. Francis school. Murphy's case is the gun that won't stop smoking. The wisp makes its way from Terry Place in Madison to St. Francis to the Milwaukee archdiocese, through priests, bishops, cardinals and finally to the current Pope Benedict, a former German cardinal named Joe Ratzinger. All of these guys had a chance to do right by our neighbor Steve Geier. None of them did.

Child rapist Larry Murphy remained a priest until the day he died in comfort at his retreat in Boulder Junction. He was never charged. Never expelled from the Catholic Church. Never defrocked. He was simply transferred to Superior, Wisconsin, the Milwaukee Diocese's version of Siberia, where he was also accused of abusing young boys.

Unlike the raped deaf boys, Larry Murphy was protected by the church. Among his protectors, suggests *The New York Times*, is Joe Ratzinger, the current Pope Benedict.

Steve wasn't the only Madison boy abused by a priest. And Larry Murphy wasn't the only Wisconsin priest using his title, authority and vestments to rape boys.

Several years ago, I was playing golf with three hometown Madison guys. All raised Catholic. The name of one specific Madison priest was mentioned. As it turns out, I was the only one in the foursome who wasn't accosted by the guy.

Guess I wasn't cute enough.

This predator's preferred means of child abuse was to convince young boys to wrestle with him in their underwear. Two of my friends had to fend off this guy at Holy Name Seminary the night before their weddings. Just how sick do you have to be to try to wrestle the groom in your underwear the night before you say his wedding mass?

The other guy and his little brother were younger when accosted by this priest. Both kids had been convinced to take off some of their clothes and wrestle the supposed holy man before the older brother, age 10, realized that something was terribly wrong. He ran from the priest, carrying his younger brother in his arms, out of the parish house and into the snow.

Two young boys, wearing nothing but underwear, running from a priest in the winter snows of Wisconsin. Wouldn't that make a nice holy card?

So, what do we make of this?

Blustery Bob Morlino (I don't like to use titles for Catholic hierarchy anymore) will probably echo the Vatican's talking points and vilify *The New York Times*, claiming Joe Ratzinger was not complicit in protecting Murphy. If he does, he will be wrong.

Indeed, the big question is that of complicity. What people were complicit in the church's wrongdoings? And who will become complicit now that new information has emerged about horrid, systemic abuse cases just made public in Ireland and Austria?

An argument could be made that the everyday Catholics and good priests in Madison who choose to dutifully participate in mass and celebrate as if nothing ever happened to Steve Geier and his deaf classmates are now supportive of the cover-up, if not complicit in it.

And that by going along as if nothing ever happened, filling the air with hollow and arcane excuses, they are pretending to be just what the pope says he is.

A good German.

02.13
HAVE A CIGAR

But there are certain birthdays that serve as important benchmarks, gauges against which you check your life.

There are birthdays, and then there are Birthdays.

When you are a child, every celebration of your arrival is exciting.

It's all about you, with balloons, cake and cards.

As you get older, birthdays, because they have begun to accumulate, matter less. In the grand scheme of things, how much does it matter that you are turning 37?

But there are certain birthdays that serve as important benchmarks, gauges against which you check your life.

You turn twenty-one. You celebrate The Adult Birthday. Of course, 21-year-olds are hardly adults. In fact, you are still an adolescent, but you can see adulthood from where you are standing. Your life as a student has ended or will soon. You will have to cut your hair, stop doing Red Bull and vodka shots at midnight, buy some business clothes and get up early in the morning. Good luck.

You turn 30. The Look in the Mirror Birthday. You confront the questions this benchmark demands: Am I on the right course for my life? Is the person I am seeing the real thing or just another dance? Am I married? Do I want to be? Do I have kids? Do I want them? Am I in the right career? Or do I want to torch my cubicle and hang my boss out the window from his/her ankles as Bud White did to the predatory district attorney in "L.A. Confidential?"

Forty is The Halftime Birthday. Actuarially speaking, you are at the halftime of your life. So you go into the locker room, take a look at the score and assess. If you are going to make any major changes, now is the time because your window of opportunity for course corrections is rapidly closing. Happy in your marriage? Comfortable with those extra 30 pounds? That third brandy every night? Like your career? If the answer is "no," you best take action soon or you are locked into the dreaded Life of Quiet Desperation to which many allude, but few admit.

Next is The Big 5-0. They blow up the black balloons, buy you a cane with a horn and welcome you, legitimately, to middle age. By this birthday your body is beginning to proclaim its age. Joint pain, hot flashes and reading glasses are your new friends. Your fiftieth birthday is there to remind you that, though you can run from Father Time, you cannot hide. At its core, this birthday is a simple, stark statement: "Hey. You aren't young. Not even close."

And then comes the benchmark facing this writer this month.

Sixty.

Sixty freaking years on the planet.

If this is the year of your sixtieth, you were born in 1953. In that year, the life expectancy for an American male was sixty-six years. Along with doo-wop music floating from a tiny radio out into the summer night, mosquito fogging and the smell of a new baseball mitt, your memory of 60 years old is of people near death.

By such standards, a sixtieth birthday should be called The Near-Death Experience.

But wait. While you were growing up they discovered that smoking isn't good for you. Neither is too much red meat and booze. Plus, they invented safer cars and statins, and they're giving cancer a run for its money. So even though you are now the age of what old and near-dead looked like when you were young, you aren't really that age. Or so you say. But if not, what age are you? How do you label the sixtieth birthday?

The word that comes to mind is "savor." By the time you're 60, there is no argument that you have lived a lot of life. Decades of marriage and relationships. Parenting. Work. By any gauge, you have done a lot.

So let us proclaim the sixtieth birthday as the Have a Cigar benchmark.

When you hit 60, take ten minutes. Put your feet up. Light a cigar, even if you have never smoked one, and congratulate yourself. One won't kill you. Laugh at the historic symmetry that a cigar is what your father presented to everyone he knew in celebration of your birth. Laugh harder knowing that he wasn't actually a witness to your arrival because back then they wouldn't let him in the delivery room with your mother, much less allow him to cut the umbilical cord.

But surely, having lived 60 years you have earned a moment to gaze on a rich sunset and savor the simple fact that you have survived six damn decades of drama, mistakes, sadness, joy, loss, confusion, passion, ambiguity, bedlam and fun.

You know…

Life.

07.13
FIRE IN THE SKY

I am smitten because they are daring, colorful, close yet distant, violent and noisy and beautiful and fun. And because they are dangerous.

Long before they produced my Apple devices, I was a big fan of the Chinese.

Because centuries prior to the smart phone and MacBook Air, they created, for all the world to enjoy … fireworks.

It is simply not possible to express in words how grateful I am to them for their fine work, because I really, really, really like fireworks.

I am smitten because they are daring, colorful, close yet distant, violent and noisy and beautiful and fun. And because they are dangerous.

My earliest fireworks memories come from sitting on a blanket at Vilas Park in the '50s. The grounds were a sea of cotton throws and families. Even before the sun set, while clans were filing in and claiming their square of grass, the noise would commence. A battery of shots would fly into the air creating the world's loudest drumroll. They would announce that the show that would begin when the sun was gone and the sky was deemed dark enough by the mysterious cannoneers who worked their fire magic on the small island near the park shelter from whence the shells took flight.

And then the first glorious shot would hit the dark night and the world would glow impossibly green and red and blue. And we would "oooh" and "aaah" as one, as if reciting litanies in church.

Other patches of grass at Westmorland and Blackhawk would also offer shows. They came with the same sense of wonder, summer, satisfaction and community. There was even drama when a shell would fire short and make its way into the crowd. There would be concern, but then the show would go on.

As I got older, I began to dabble in fireworks shows myself. Nothing to match Terry Kelly's fine work, more like a garage project. It began on our cul-de-sac when the kids were young. I spirited away to one of the roadside stands that pop up around the Fourth like mushrooms in the woods. Bought some small displays, mostly fountains, a few aerials and whistlers.

The second year of my little production, Neighbor Jon asked me to briefly delay the start. He left the yard, then returned five minutes later, silently directing everyone's attention to his house, where he had placed lawn sprinklers on his shake cedar roof. He then nodded for me to begin the show.

Now most of our Fourth fireworks activity occurs north at the lake. Last year the bevy of our kids' friends decided to put on a small display while sitting at the new fire pit they had just dug. Two shells fired first, both small and nondescript. But the third took off high into the sky in glorious fashion and exploded overhead. Then, as if guided by the Gods of Fire, a trailing shell ember plummeted to earth and landed directly in the fire pit, setting off a secondary yet harmless explosion. The gang sat stunned, and then erupted in applause at this amazing, true baptism by fire.

But my favorite fireworks memory came on a Fourth some ten years ago. By now there was serious production involved. I played the soundtrack from Ken Burns' *The Civil War* from the speakers of my car. Created a launch pad with a deck table and a plank of plywood. Purchased large shells and fountains at the local bait shop, where I was confidentially informed by the guy behind the counter with a knowing nod that the fireworks were "from Arkansas." Ever-responsible bride Diane cleared everyone away to a distance of 30 yards. She had the garden hose at the ready. I donned protective glasses.

I began the show with the simultaneous ignition of three large ground fountains. They were tame but fun as, like small volcanoes, they threw their many colors 20 feet into the air.

The faces of family and friends gathered on the summer night lawn were lit in brilliance. Then, suddenly, as if possessed, brother Bobby (always the most daring of the Roach boys) took off on a dead run and ran straight through the wall of sparks yelling at the top of his lungs, "God Bless America!!!"

Perhaps it was unwise. But for a brief moment, in a freeze frame, Bobby became part of the fireworks. He WAS a firework.

Bobby emerged unharmed and exhilarated, though chastened by his wife. When I asked him why he made his sparkling dash he just shrugged, "It seemed like the right thing to do at the time."

WHILE I HAVE YOUR ATTENTION

So on this Fourth, be careful. Enjoy the beauty and wonder of fireworks. Honor our country.

And take a moment to thank the Chinese.

01.16
A MANY SPLENDORED THING

Not since the Pill has something changed the American romantic landscape in such stunning fashion.

The scene is a family wedding. The young and old are gathered to wish the happy couple the very best.

At the lively reception—a whirlwind of emotion, sound and joy—the conversation at our table turns to the love lives of the single young adults seated with us.

And the big question seems to be: Tinder or Match.com?

All of the 20- and 30-somethings here have dabbled in online dating, a modern phenomenon alien to many of the previous generations. Some of have found sweethearts. Many of their friends have found marriage partners.

Not since the Pill has something changed the American romantic landscape in such stunning fashion.

Lest we forget, the birth control pill was truly revolutionary (even for Catholics). With the simple daily ingestion of this miracle drug, the likelihood and willingness to become pregnant could now be managed. By women.

This small pill has had astounding ramifications. First, it boldly presented the notion that women might want to have sex for reasons other than procreation.

Imagine that.

The Pill also profoundly changed marriage. Women could now delay childbearing and pursue careers. Women developed careers so successful or necessary it sent many of them back to work after childbirth, thus changing the way we raise our kids.

And the Pill made families smaller. In the near-west-side Madison neighborhood in which I was raised, there were families with eight, 11 and 13 children. Kids had astounding independence simply because there were too many of us to monitor. A "helicopter parent" meant your dad was a pilot.

Today, families of that size are nearly extinct.

And now comes another revolution in mating in the form of digital dating. Rather than meeting at school, work, church or in a bar, young singles, and more adventurous older ones, can meet on their computers, phones and iPads via dating sites, augmented by texting, Snapchat, FaceTime and just about any app that lets people communicate.

What are we to think of this? On the plus side, the web allows you to research your dates. You can run CCAP reports to see if there are any felonies in their past. You can check them out via Facebook and Twitter to make sure they aren't married. You can add qualifiers to your potential mates on the dating apps, thus reducing the number you want to audition, all while casting a must wider net than you could in your town a generation ago.

And then after meeting via app, texting and FaceTime, you can actually rendezvous in a physical place and stand in actual proximity to this person to determine if this real human being is anything like the virtual one you presume to know.

It is easy for an older generation to be cynical about such things, but I know too many young people who have found love this way to scoff at it. And why should we?

Why should the unrelenting drive for most humans to engage in pair bonding be limited to the people who just so happen to live in your town, go to your school or work at the same place as you? From a purely scientific standpoint, this old model severely limits how many you choose to swim with in the gene pool.

But what is most striking is the issue of control. In the past, true love seemed like happenstance—a lightning bolt, parental wishes or simple comfort over time. But now it is a thoughtful, exacting search, with specific criteria communicated to the world as to who might interest you.

And it causes you to ponder, as Aziz Ansari has done in his book, "Modern Romance," that millennial singles may now have too many options, paralyzing romance for a generation.

Of course, there will always be those who want to kick old school by quaffing three beers and mustering the courage to wander up to that cute one and start a conversation.

But no matter the method, it is remarkable, even beautiful, to see how humans work so hard to invent so many intriguing ways that just might allow them to meet the person they can love.

For we all are driven, not just to procreate, but to find that someone to share our bed each night, perhaps forever, as we seek shelter from the storm.

02.17
TAKE A KNEE

While the air was filled with bluster, insults and bellowing, this man spoke in quiet tones and with one simple act.

Some of those with a flag on their jacket also think they are uniquely qualified to determine who else is a patriot and who isn't, ignorant of the fact that some of the least patriotic citizens in our history have wrapped themselves in the flag while walking all over our Constitution.

Amidst the most partisan and acrimonious election in decades, if not centuries, there was one man in America who made a political statement in a different way.

While the air was filled with bluster, insults and bellowing, this man spoke in quiet tones and with one simple act.

That man was San Francisco 49ers football player Colin Kaepernick.

On Sept. 1, 2016, before the 49ers' last exhibition game against the San Diego Chargers, Kaepernick went to one knee as the national anthem began. He later explained his action to reporters: "I am not going to stand up to show pride for a country that oppresses black people and people of color. To me, this is bigger than football and it would be selfish on my part to look the other way. There are bodies in the street and people getting paid leave and getting away with murder."

Kaepernick's act and words incensed many. He was broadly condemned by irate patriots who called him a coward, loser and much worse. But these fellow citizens, though entitled to their opinions, might not be as right as they think they are.

First, the NFL exploits patriotism in the cheesiest form of borrowed equity ever practiced. Sure, there is a lump in the throat as the fighter jets fly by while the last anthem notes soar and the flag covers the entire field, but there is something false about all the pageantry.

Standing on any given NFL field are some of the strongest, fastest, toughest men in our country. Yet, as best as we can currently tell, out of the 53-man rosters of the NFL's 32 teams, only Alejandro Villenueva of the Pittsburgh Steelers has served in the U.S. military. That means the NFL percentage of military veterans is 0.05896 percent.

So … how patriotic is that?

Second, regarding the charge of cowardice, there are few things short of combat that require more physical courage and mental toughness than playing in the NFL, especially in the quarterback position. If those accusing Kaepernick of cowardice were forced to play in an NFL game, they would go fetal on the first play and remain in said position until the bleachers were being cleaned.

There is also the general assumption that if you wear a flag on your lapel and sing the anthem loudest that you are more patriotic than the next citizen. Some of those with a flag on their jacket also think they are uniquely qualified to determine who else is a patriot and who isn't, ignorant of the fact that some of the least patriotic citizens in our history have wrapped themselves in the flag while walking all over our Constitution. Joe McCarthy and your average KKK member come to mind.

One of the other rapid responses toward Kaepernick has been the accusation that he is showing disrespect for the members of our armed forces. Kaepernick, who graduated from high school with a 4.0 GPA, has thoughtfully and patiently explained how he holds servicemen and women in high regard. If you take that charge against Kaepernick to its logical conclusion, then any protest is an act of disrespect toward veterans, never mind that the birth of our nation, flag and anthem resulted from an act of protest.

And then there is the motivation behind Kaepernick's act: justice for all.

It is shocking how scads of white folk, who have never lived in a black neighborhood, lob withering attacks at Kaepernick without ever considering that being black in America is not always a pleasant thing, and that injustices occur with regularity, sometimes with fatal results. Open any American history book. We have a long record of viewing black lives as disposable.

And finally, there is the concept of freedom. The fact that Kaepernick can kneel in protest without being imprisoned or executed by the state is the greatest beauty of America. That very freedom is what our servicemen and women actually protect. And yet so many bellow when that freedom is actually practiced.

So, as the Super Bowl and its theatrics loom before us, remember that when the anthem is sung and the B-1 bombers fly overhead, you are perfectly within your rights to remain seated on your couch. Smart, good Americans, all residents of the land of the free and home of the brave, will think nothing less of you.

God Bless America.

02.18
NO PARTICULAR PLACE TO GO

This is a stress response that I have long pondered: Get in the car and drive. Jump on a train and see where it takes you.

Recent circumstances required me to clear my head. When I was a younger man that meant a five-mile run. Age has made that a lost alternative, so I tried something I've never done. Something that sounds old but wasn't at all.

I took a drive in the country.

This is a stress response that I have long pondered: Get in the car and drive. Jump on a train and see where it takes you.

So, on this day I drove. It was wonderful to see where my car went.

With no plan, I headed west past Verona and Mount Horeb, to Barneveld — the "Town that Blew Away."

For those new to the area, in June 1984, this small farming town was visited by one of the most powerful F5 tornadoes to ever touch ground in the United States. Barneveld was utterly destroyed. Thirteen lives were lost and many more changed forever.

But I knew the town before the Big Wind came. In 1970, before my junior year in high school, I signed on to bail hay and do chores at the Bunbury dairy farm just outside of Barneveld. The thought was that it would make me stronger for football, but the benefits proved to be far greater than bigger biceps.

The farm had been in the Bunbury family for generations. Tom and Marijo Bunbury, a young couple just out of college with a baby, were then running it for the family. Tom, now a successful real estate magnate, had grown up in Madison and attended Edgewood High School while living the dual life of a farm boy.

For two summers I carried milk pails, drove a tractor, stacked hay bales on a wagon and again in the mow. Tom and Marijo were patient with me. If nothing else I was comic relief as I learned the ways of manure and sweat. It was, quite simply, the purest form of work I have ever done.

And now, for some reason, my car was taking me back there.

I find the land of southwest Wisconsin to have a beauty that rivals the rural vistas of France and Ireland. The rolling hills, the wooded dales with bedded deer that dot every farm. And over all of it stand the great Blue Mounds.

The drive took place on a warm first week of this past December. The crops were in and the sun was bright. The brown, stubbled fields yet to be covered in snow added a golden hue to everything. The low December sun made it magic hour all day.

It had been 47 years since I last visited the farm. The fear was that I wouldn't find it, but, like a bell cow to the barn, my car headed to the right place. My SUV drove through the web of trunk roads directly to the Bunburys' driveway.

Just seeing it took my breath away. It allowed me to think about when I was young, and the independence that drove me to leave town in summer to work as a hired hand — an interesting move for a young guy, and a precursor to other moves in my life.

I lingered at the entrance to the farm. I took a few pictures. And then I decided to keep driving. I checked Google and discovered that there were only 30 miles of farm roads between me and Mineral Point, a town that I have passed but never visited. So I did. I idled by Pendarvis and the old mining homes still clinging to the steep hills. I took a selfie on the main street to send to my buddy Mike who grew up there.

It was still light, so I looked at my phone and found that it was only another 30 miles of back road to get to another interesting town, Spring Green. So, I drove there, too, marveling at the towering hills and cliffs that announced the entrance to the Wisconsin River Valley and Taliesin, a part of our state known by all the world.

The sun was fading. I headed home, freed from the consternation that drove me to the road by the pure, timeless beauty of the lands just outside our town, and the perspective provided by the memory.

A wag once wrote, "The worst thing about getting old is remembering when you were young."

But on this day, on the quiet farm roads of Wisconsin, those memories weren't bad at all.

In fact, they were reassuring and comforting. As was the freedom of just getting in the car and seeing where it would take me.

So, when in doubt, drive.

04.18
WORKING ARTIST

These are men and women who live among us and do something that isn't easy: They make a living in the arts.

We are in a tavern in Stoughton.

There is a Viking canoe just off to our right with smoke wafting from the nose of the dragon on its bow. These Norwegians are absolutely crazy.

Our gaggle has gathered to attend a concert at the Stoughton Opera House, as fine a little entertainment venue as you will ever enjoy.

We have come to watch a group of working Madison musicians do their thing in homage to a band for the ages: Steely Dan. The Madison act smartly calls itself Steely Dane. My millennial daughters jumped in at the last moment to join us. Seems they like "My Old School," too.

For two hours, 10 of us sing from the balcony as the musicians slay the work of Donald Fagen and Walter Becker. The maestro and chief arranger, Dave Adler, cavorts about the stage. Behind him, Dave Stoler, Thomas Mattioli, Phil Lyons and others bring the groove and funk as Biff Blumfumgagne, Al Falashci, Jay Moran, Courtney Larsen and others take turns singing lead vocals. The large ensemble fills the hall with soul and smarts.

It is a big band with a big sound, and it is damn near perfect.

For some reason I am truly moved by the work of these musicians. These are men and women who live among us and do something that isn't easy: They make a living in the arts. Some of them augment their cash flow with day jobs as teachers, computer programmers and the like. But on this night, on that stage, they seemed to be doing exactly what they were meant to be doing with their lives.

Being artists.

Making a living in the arts is a tricky proposition. It's the news parents don't want to get from their kids upon college graduation. It's a high-risk proposition when they announce they want to act, sing, play, compose, write or draw.

For more than four decades the arts have been my lot, both commercially and otherwise. I've counseled a lot of young folks on whether to pursue an artistic career, always telling them to take their shot—because if they don't, it will haunt them. And if they fail, and they have to follow a straighter occupational route, they will be shocked at how much they learned as a working artist, with a body of knowledge and experience that can be applied to any business field.

But I always tell them to try.

Because whatever they are feeling, the life of an artist is calling to them. They have to heed that call while they are young and free of a spouse, offspring and a mortgage. If they don't heed it, all they will own is regret.

A life in the arts is viewed by many as risky, because so many folks view it as an all-or-nothing play. You go to Hollywood and you become Jennifer Lawrence or Ryan Gosling, or not. But the arts offer much more opportunity than the palm trees of Hollywood.

Madison is full of agencies and departments that pay artists to write, direct, draw, edit, design or photograph. According to the National Endowment for the Arts, there are more than 2.1 million workers employed nationally in the arts, with a high percentage of them being self-employed entrepreneurs.

In my early life I had a lot of different jobs. Some of them were fun. Some weren't. But none compared to the moment I got my first job as a writer. Ever since that day decades ago, I've never looked at a clock at work.

So many folks spend their lives, in Jackson Brown's words, struggling "for the legal tender," doing work that they endure for the sake of family and lifestyle. But in their hearts, it's not much more than a mercenary act.

But then there are others who get to do the work they are meant to do.

And that's the way it looked for the artists at the Stoughton Opera House. None of them were watching the clock. They were having too much fun.

When waxing about working in the arts to friends, staff or students, I always fall back to a line I like.

I tell folks that, like the gang in Steely Dane, I'm lucky. Because, as a working artist, what I do is who I am.

How great is that?

THE CONFUSED MIDDLE

The moral tension is enough to make the average person wretch.

06.04
MY FELLOW AMERICANS

Such an act is stunning in its disregard for every gay American who is a brother, sister, daughter, son, co-worker, friend or parent.

Jen has been working with our group for the last five years. Although she started out as an office manager, she is now a senior producer, handling some of our most prestigious accounts. I have met few people who are as smart, conscientious and well-adjusted as Jen.

By any standard, Jen is an Above-Average American.

In fact, when we are out for beers with the work gang, I like to kid Jen and tell her that from now on I am hiring only lesbians.

Jen laughs when I say this.

But she has not been laughing much these days.

Steve is one of the smartest guys I have ever met. A cracker-jack lawyer, innovative thinker, wit and counsel to powerful men. Again, by any standard he is an Above-Average American.

He is also, to my knowledge, the only gay member of our Friday afternoon Avenue Bar group. We like to crack wise and discuss the issues of the day. Steve had an interesting quote the other day when asked about who he is supporting in the presidential election.

"Neither. There is no difference," he answered bitterly. "One calls me 'nigger,' the other calls me 'colored.'"

This year someone has decided, in one of the most venal political acts ever engineered, to make the emerging gay marriage issue this election's political litmus test.

Such an act is stunning in its disregard for every gay American who is a brother, sister, daughter, son, co-worker, friend or parent. As women and black Americans have done in our past, they are simply asserting their rights and freedom. It is the American Way.

Smarter and more patriotic citizens must tell these gay baiters to shut up and sit down. Average Americans, who honor freedom and all it stands for, must put these ignorant knuckleheads in their place, just as we did with Joe McCarthy and Bull Connor decades ago.

And I am just the Average American to do it!

Actually, I can solve this for everyone. This time next year my wife Diane and I will be celebrating our 25th wedding anniversary. Ergo, I am as qualified as George Bush, Congress, our goofball state legislators and the pope to hold forth on the institution of marriage and who should be allowed to wed.

First, let's deal with sex. It seems to me that everyone is just too damn hung up on it.

As anyone who has been married for 25 years can testify, marriage isn't about sex.

It's about talking negotiating, laughing, money, food, the bills, the kids, companionship, community, the dog, the lawn, the furnace filters, quarrels, groceries, the snow tires, taxes, health insurance and taking care of the other one when they have a fever.

And then … when all of that is taken care of … and if you're lucky … there might be time for a little nooky. And if you have been married for 25 years you don't really care what kind of sex anyone else is having — so long as your teenagers are not having it yet.

And what of the issue of kids, and the question of whether or not homosexuals can be fit parents?

I have seen hetero-marrieds run screaming onto a soccer field filled with eight-year-olds because they didn't like the referee, pile five toddlers into the back seat of a car and never buckle a seat belt, and abandon their wife and children for the secretary.

So much for us.

Here are the questions gays should be asked to see if they are fit to be parents.

Are you capable of wiping up vomit?

Tying shoes over and over again?

Loving kids relentlessly even when that love is not instantly returned?

If you answer "yes" to all three, you can be a parent.

And what of the legal rights of gay Americans? Well, let's see. Gay Americans pay taxes, vote, serve in the military. In fact, one could surmise that as long as there has been an America, there have been gay Americans, fighting and dying for the very rights they are now being denied.

There is no doubt that there have been gay Medal of Honor winners, an honor no goof in the Wisconsin State Legislature has ever earned.

In fact, it's a pretty good bet that there has been a gay president.

My guess is Millard Fillmore. I think he might be have been a lesbian. But I may be wrong.

Finally, let this Average American guy, veteran of 25 years of marriage, say that I don't think gay unions undermine marriage at all. In fact, I think the fact that hundreds of thousands of gay partners want to marry actually elevates and honors the proposition. Far more than Liz Taylor ever did. I wish all my gay friends good luck and hope they find a partner as good as mine.

And finally, one last word from this Average American to the politicians and religious rightists who have made my friends and fellow Americans Jen and Steve feel so sad.

Shame on you.

04.07
EVIL BONES ON A COLD MUD FLOOR

For years, I have had pangs of Catholic American guilt for driving a gas eater.

I turn the key, and nothing happens.

And it is comforting.

The first thing you notice when you drive a hybrid car, at least the one I purchased, is that it remains nearly silent when it starts. After decades of a throaty, gas-guzzling roar, the quiet electric hum is cognitive dissonance I haven't experienced since sampling clear beer.

Just a simple white signal winks at you from the dash and says, "Ready."

Funny, because when it comes to oil and the Middle East, our leaders have been anything but ready.

For years I have had pangs of Catholic American guilt for driving a gas eater.

Further, I just felt plain stupid.

This guilt had less to do with Al Gore and global warming, a long-term problem that we are just now confronting.

No, I felt stupid because I was ignoring a more immediate problem: the growing horde of ignorant, suicidal, religio-fascists of the Middle

East, the hateful mullahs who exhort them in the name of a twisted, violent god, and the billionaire tribal kings who serve as their dictators from a top-floor suite, packed with blonde escorts and single malt, at Caesar's Palace.

Like many Americans, despite the ill-informed and poorly executed attempt to occupy Iraq, I accept the notion that we are in a greater war against a sick, global brotherhood of Islamic terrorists.

And I would like to do something to help in this fight.

But the only folks who have been asked to do anything by our president and Congress are the volunteers of our armed services.

Our Army, Marine and National Guard folks who are sent out daily as IED bait.

So we, the insulated, continue to get gas for our cars.

While our young servicemen and women get prosthetic devices.

Or a full military funeral.

As political satirist Bill Maher so bluntly put it... "Why isn't our President making them fight ALL of us?" Good question, Billy.

Something has seemed terribly out of whack since 9/11.

Just a few days after the attack, our Mumbler-in-Chief posed for pix with a suave, blazer-wearing Saudi prince in the Oval Office. They were chuckling. I wondered what could be so funny given the fact that sixteen of the eighteen hijackers were from the prince's neighborhood.

How that oily prince made "w" (he has lost his right to uppercase) laugh, while the towers and bodies beneath still smoldered, I will never know.

Instead of trading secret frat handshakes with a Saudi prince, why wasn't the Fourth Brightest Member of the Bush Family cutting to the chase and challenging America to use our ingenuity and national will to kick our sand fluid habit, thus making all of us less vulnerable to its associated Islamic madness?

In the wake of 9/11, we would have done anything.

Gasless Sundays. Ride sharing. Push mowers. Something.

But you know what "w" asked us to do? Nothing.

When I pulled into my buddy's driveway he chuckled at my hybrid, claiming the gas savings would not pay for its premium cost for more than five years.

I told him that wasn't the point.

The point was about making a point.

I want the dullards in Detroit and Congress and the Oval Office to know that we want to use as little as possible of Islam's black crack. We want market demand to force automakers to make even better hybrids so that the ignorant, violent elements of the Middle East eventually become inconsequential to our families and our communities.

Islamic fundamentalists are like the crazy relatives at a wedding.

You are never going to change them. So just avoid them.

And if tooling around in my hybrid also helps stem global warming, great!

I can then rightfully be a Republican Patriot and a Democratic-Progressive-Dane-Save-the-Earth cat at the same time.

How cool is that?

Plus, Larry David will wave at me.

There is a three-block stretch on Monroe street where the hybrid hums along at 30 and proudly informs the driver that he is getting 99 miles to the gallon. At this moment I imagine Al Gore smiling smarmily … but better yet, I fantasize that somewhere in a cave in the mountainous region of Pakistan someone whispers this news to Osama bin Laden. And it makes his evil bones shift uncomfortably on the cold, mud floor that is his mattress.

I turn the key, and nothing happens.

And it feels great.

01.12
THE CONFUSED MIDDLE

Just when all seems lost, he is offered redemption with one last chance to fight for an excruciatingly elusive goal: justice.

We live in a time of moral confusion. In the last year we have been buffeted by constant acrimony.

RECALL WALKER! STOP THE EDGEWATER! OPPOSE MADISON PREP! Or SUPPORT WALKER! BACK THE EDGEWATER! SUPPORT MADISON PREP!

These controversies, and the issues swirling in their wake, have made a difficult year for any person of conscience. It has shaken our belief in ourselves. We fear that we can no longer talk, negotiate and proceed without vitriol. Or lobbing a Hitler metaphor.

We have become Frank Galvin, a character played masterfully by Paul Newman in *The Verdict*. Galvin was a fine man, but the sheer pain of life led him to drink and crash. Just when all seems lost, he is offered redemption with one last chance to fight for an excruciatingly elusive goal: justice.

In his summation, the underdog Galvin, weighted by despair, begins with quiet words to the jury. *You know, so much of the time we're just lost. We say, "Please, God, tell us what is right; tell us what is true." And there is no justice: the rich win; the poor are powerless. We become tired of hearing people lie. And after a time, we become … a little dead. We think of ourselves as victims … and we become victims.*

In Madison, the rancor has worn us down. It seems damn near impossible to determine what is just and true while drums bang and the smarmy politicians, exploitive media and flush lobbyists blare in our ears like vuvuzelas.

But there is a standard that a former Catholic boy is trying to use as criteria. It is a platform that transcends conservative vs. liberal definitions. It is the concept of social justice, a value shared across many faiths and political ideologies. The core of this philosophy is twofold: respect the dignity of each person and, when in doubt, show preference toward the poor or most vulnerable.

These criteria will anger some. No surprise. Right now, Wisconsin has more anger than field corn and more victims than cheese curds.

But let us proceed nonetheless. Using this standard, the first persons voted off Justice Island are anyone associated with Wall Street and banking. They drove us off the cliff while being paid ridiculous sums. Sure, they help maintain a free market, but they failed to do it responsibly. They should remain quiet — and happy they aren't joining the conversation on a cell, from a cell.

The next to be ignored are politicians. This call is easy. Both parties are (to borrow a word from Michael Moore) awash in lobbyist money. Which takes us to lobbyists. It doesn't matter if it is WEAC cash or Koch coin, their lucre is being delivered in dump trucks to sway votes.

They have immense amounts of cash and they use it in every election to obtain power. Ignore them.

Now comes the morally confusing part: the rest of us. Like a final episode of "Survivor," events have conspired to pit friends against each other. Today unprotected private sector workers seem to be vying for justice against state workers who, though secure, are hardly wealthy.

The Edgewater debate posed another justice question. Can you help a decimated business sector and local construction industry with tax incentives when the city is strapped, and cops and firemen are taking wage freezes?

The concept of Madison Prep gets even more confusing. How do you weigh the rights of children and families of poverty and color against the position of an already embattled teacher corps, many of whom spend much of their lives helping those very kids in jeopardy?

The moral tension is enough to make the average person wretch.

Complicating all of this is the relative comfort most of us have enjoyed. This economy requires sacrifice anyone born after 1930 has never, ever pondered. In other times Americans sold apples on street corners to feed their families. Or endured the rationing of sugar and gasoline. But now, as one person protested hysterically to me, "We have had to give up our season tickets to American Players Theatre!" From a historical perspective, my dear, this is not sacrifice.

So how do we decide on what is right? Well, I have reached a position with a qualification. I choose not to demonize those with whom I disagree, because I know these times suck for pretty much everyone. In the end, I will make decisions according to my new, incredibly complicated formula for justice: C-M-L=J. Or, the Cause with the Least Money and Fewest Lawyers Gets Justice. Frank Galvin's final words offer us hope that we can do this. *If we are to have faith in justice, we need only to believe in ourselves. And act with justice. See, I believe there is justice in our hearts.*

Of course, this leaves me with another confusion headache. Frank Galvin, the character played by Paul Newman? He was a lawyer.

05.12
BANG, BANG

We have all sorts of other things in abundance. Can't we shoot them first?

Well, it's about time we get to shoot some new things.

For decades, the good, binge-drinking people of Wisconsin have had to be content with shooting deer, squirrels, woodcock and grouse.

But now they're talking about letting us shoot the few wolves we have managed to reintroduce into the state. Plus, we may get to stalk another aggressive creature, the dreaded and ferocious sandhill crane.

The sandhill, or as I like to call it, *grus canadensisis*, is a large bird that has recently made a comeback in these parts. In the spring you can hear its ancient call, a sound every bit as haunting as the cry of the loon. They are a large, absolutely beautiful bird.

One of the last things you consider when you see one is, "Wow, I would really like to shoot that thing." And yet, that is just what your poorly dressed lawmakers at the Capitol are considering.

They also want us to shoot wolves.

The majestic and functional wolf, adept at controlling the deer population, is finally beginning to thrive after we spent decades and millions of dollars reintroducing them to their natural habitat in the northern reaches of the state.

I have actually seen a wolf. It was a lone creature, romping over first ice on one of the large lakes outside Minocqua. It, too, was beautiful. Again, it never crossed my mind to dispatch it with a high-powered rifle. Or chase it down with a pack of dogs and an ATV.

Aaaaand now cue the NRA. I can hear them huffing, so let me assure you that I have been hunting. And I have shot pistols. Not a big deal. And I absolutely understand the notion of subsistence hunting and fishing so important to families in our state. Let's face it, our plentiful whitetails are fine and valuable protein on the hoof.

But, really, aren't we getting a little gun happy in Wisconsin?

We lead the nation in morbid obesity. Do we really need to add sandhill cranes to our crowded diet?

And we only have 800 wolves in the state. That is effectively the same number as annual high school national merit scholars, and we haven't declared a season on them. Yet.

We have all sorts of other things in abundance. Can't we shoot them first?

Let's have a season on dairy cows. Family pets. People who insist on driving fifty-nine miles per hour in the passing lane. Chicago Bears fans. Women wearing tight, low-slung, thong-revealing jeans who shouldn't. Men who beat women. Smokers.

And, of course, let's shoot high school students who drink beer in the spring.

Which, by all accounts is what happened to Bo Morrison.

Bo was a 20-year-old kid from Slinger. He was not a national merit scholar, but he had just enlisted in the United State Marine Corps to protect and serve us. Bo was at an underage beer party when a neighbor called the cops. As kids all over Wisconsin do when the cops are called, they scattered to avoid a ticket and parental wrath. I personally know one very smart kid who spent the night on a neighbor's roof in an attempt to dodge the cops and the scar on his reputation.

At any rate, an unarmed, probably tipsy Bo Morrison ran and hid on a nearby porch. The porch owner, Adam Kind, who knew the cops were in the neighborhood, heard someone outside. Instead of shouting the kid away, or yelling to the police next door, Mr. Kind stepped onto his porch and shot Bo Morrison once in the chest with a .45-caliber handgun, killing him.

The unarmed Bo Morrison could have been a thug, rapist or murderer. But a felon picking a home 300 feet away from the police squad cars to create mayhem would have to be very, very stupid.

Which, interestingly enough, is what the shooter, Adam Kind, is. Stupid.

Not a sandhill crane. Nor a wolf. Adam Kind got to bag himself a human being.

The law in our state allows Mr. Kind to shoot kids from a spring beer party if they are on his property. The laws in our state also allow you to wander in an open field during a lightning storm with a three iron over your head.

But just because you can do it doesn't mean you should.

Adam Kind took an incredibly bad shot. Bad in a moral way. Bad in an NRA way.

If all the police in our state were as stupid as Adam Kind, we'd have 500 high school kids dead by gunshot every spring.

But, hey, this is Wisconsin. We are fat, drunk and armed.

Which presents a fun, Hunger Games kind of idea.

Let's put all our mean, stupid, untrained, paranoid, phallically challenged gun folks in the woods for one weekend.

And let them hunt each other.

After all, it's Wisconsin. We love something new to shoot.

06.12
STORM WARNING

So, the wall cloud appeared on the horizon. The funnel was sighted.

The bad times continue in our state, rushing soon to recall conclusion.

Everyone knows the special election won't do much for healing.

That process will take much longer.

Even now, many of us are still staggering around like tornado victims crawling out from our basements after the winds have passed.

We numbly ask, "What the hell happened? How did we get here?"

The quickest take is to blame Mr. Walker. Like a political cyclone, he blew into Madison and the landscape changed. But that is too easy.

Many factors go into a tornado. The event requires terrifying calculus.

In the case of Wisconsin, the Gulf Stream of economics created global instability in the atmosphere, with guilt enough for both national political parties and a revenue shock to our state.

Our ground zero TORCON conditions also required hot, moist air provided by the Dems, colliding with cold, dry air provided by the Republicans.

Further, our storm preparedness was poor. The previous governor, a fellow named Jim Doyle, seemed to favor the Louis XV strategy: *après moi le deluge.* Translation: *after me the flood.* No politician has ever been so silent as Mr. Doyle of late. When the storm hit, the sirens were silent.

There were no public shelters to provide haven.

So, the wall cloud appeared on the horizon. The funnel was sighted. And then … it hit.

Some fled to cellars, others to Rockford. But Madison became a political Barneveld, destroyed by a partisan F5. The national media quickly descended to gawk at us in our wreckage.

And now they return to ogle again.

Many of us in the confused middle wonder what we will do when we get behind the polling curtains. We know teachers and state workers. They are our friends and family. But we also know how difficult this economy has been for many private-sector citizens and wonder if our pain is understood.

Either way, we all long for healing, because we think that what is happening in Wisconsin is not who we are.

This hits very close to home for me. My dad worked for, and eventually owned, a small business named Badger Sporting Goods that did work with every high school in the state from New Holstein to Cumberland to Wittenberg-Birnamwood to Bonduel.

For 40 years, John Roach Sr. met with teachers, coaches and administrators daily to determine how many track hurdles, basketballs and football helmets they could afford in their annual budget. He and his Badger Sports cohorts would host annual steak fries for the teachers and coaches who descended on Madison for the state basketball tournament. It was always a celebration in our household. We rooted for every high school in the tournament.

After all, Dad sold them their jerseys.

Some of the coaches and teachers were, and still are, my Dad's closest friends. Legendary guys with nicknames like Boob, Knobby and Weenie.

But, no surprise, there were others he worked with who were jerks.

It is a luxury for a man my age to still have his Dad around for advice. So I called him about the recall election.

"Well, I'm an independent, Johnny. But I'll tell you this," Dad said. "They should pay the good teachers more. And they should be able to fire the bad teachers. Simple as that. They're doing that in Oconomowoc. Every good teacher in the state is going to want to work there."

Dad remembers the Hortonville teachers' strike and the repercussions it had around the state. It was a tough time. Dad doesn't pretend to be pro-union.

But he likes teachers.

"You can't pay a good teacher enough," Dad said.

Maybe that is as good a motivation as one can find when entering the recall booth this month. Despite the rancor and toxicity, maybe a person can try to cast a vote to pay good teachers more. Whatever that vote be.

And then, after exiting the polling booth, look to the western sky.

Because only a fool would think that there aren't more storms on the way.

10.17
WHITE ON RICE

Let's imagine, for an unbearable moment, that America was as white as a neo-Nazi pot roast tailgate in a Chick-fil-A parking lot.

In the past weeks, we were forced to watch khaki-clad white boys waddle down the street in Charlottesville, Virginia, with $3.99 Home Depot Tiki torches held preposterously above their empty heads. After their rally for white supremacy, one of them killed a white woman with his car, which seems grossly off-strategy for a white superiority movement.

Let us set aside, if possible, the sheer hatred and ignorance of their cause. Let's forget their self-pitying whine of white oppression so pathetic in its weakness.

And let's forget, for the moment, that not one of these guys has presumably ever satisfied a woman.

Instead, let us imagine the awful place America would be if their sick wish came true.

Let's imagine, for an unbearable moment, that America was as white as a neo-Nazi pot roast tailgate in a Chick-fil-A parking lot. Mayonnaise would be our national fruit. Everything we eat would fit between white bread. Our dancing would be arrhythmic and asexual. High school kids would form committees to not have a dance because it would be just too awkward.

Every running back in the NFL would be white. As would all the wide receivers. All of them. As a former white halfback and wideout myself, I have no trepidation saying that an all-white NFL would be as inert and dull as lard. As for a solely white NBA, well, such a prospect is too horrifying to ponder.

And our culture? Polka music would dominate the airwaves. Let that sink in for a little bit. Polka.

Whose songs would serenade us? What would our world be like without Miles Davis, Sam Cooke, Chuck Berry, Marvin Gaye, Billie Holiday, Aretha Franklin, Whitney Houston and Beyoncé? Without Harold Melvin and the Blue Notes, Earth Wind and Fire, Nelly or Prince? Are you kidding me?

Think about it. When you turned on the radio, you would only hear The Six Fat Dutchmen.

Our neo-Nazi friends also have an issue with Jewish folks. Which is funny because their movement thrives on the internet; a system which was organized by two Jewish guys — Sergey Brin and Larry Page — who invented Google, which pretty much drives the whole damn world. And their dominant search engine serves devices conceived and created by Steve Jobs, the son of a Syrian refugee. Let's repeat that — a Syrian refugee.

If these guys were true white supremacists, they would refuse to use any device or system associated with what they perceive to be lesser races, which would force them to communicate by yodeling to each other from nearby hilltops.

It's tough to feel racially superior while yodeling. It just is.

These white boys also don't like Latinos, as if they are somehow outsiders, when in fact, Latinos beat all white people to America.

Latinos founded Los Angeles! It's home to Hollywood and all the action movies white boys ever loved. If it weren't for Hollywood, every American film would be shot in Texas and would end up looking like "Walker, Texas Ranger," which makes you more stupid every time you watch it. Which actually explains a lot about these guys.

Also, how would these doughy, white supremacists find the energy to march if it wasn't for Taco Bell?

Most importantly, if America were pure white, we wouldn't be America.

The very thing that makes us the most powerful, prosperous nation in world history is that we are not inbred. Our strength and brilliance come from diverse sources from all over the world. It is not a coincidence that we are back-to-back world war champions against monochromatic countries.

Why? Because America is the wonderful, colorful, brilliant opposite of inbred.

We are all born of dreamers, who live in a land of dreams. Dreams that will never be extinguished by weak, petty men.

Look. I am a white male myself. I've spent a lot of time with white people. Trust me. We are not that fun. Or interesting.

This reality reveals the ultimate, irrefutable truth of what a White America would be.

We would all be dead within a generation.

And the cause?

Sheer boredom.

WHEN NOTHING BECOMES SOMETHING

Maybe it's when you are doing nothing
at all that you get the most done.

07.04
WHEN NOTHING BECOMES SOMETHING

Most days we seem obsessed with jamming as much activity into our lives as possible, especially on our days "off."

I awoke this weekend with a stunning realization.

The heavy, biblical rains that have hammered Dane County were at it again. Ergo, no golf and male camaraderie, but, on the other hand, five reclaimed hours.

Also, no long bike ride to Mount Horeb to keep the thumper strong. Two more hours found.

I sip my morning coffee and listen to easy morning music and come to the giddy conclusion that for the next two days, my schedule is totally, utterly empty. To make things even simpler, the bride is up north with her sisters. I will miss the dear woman, but it means one less opinion concerning agenda, and thus a simpler day.

By the time my youngest makes his way down the stairs mid-morning, I am ready to pose a question for which I have become famous in our household.

"Mornin', Dad."

"Mornin', Son. Guess what we have on the schedule this weekend?"

JT smiles at the query, waits a beat, then asks, "Nothing?"

I nod gravely. "Exactly."

And so, with nothing to do, I prepare breakfast for my son. Next down the stairs comes his older sister, our high school graduate. The two of them sit at the island in the kitchen and laugh as I juggle all the elements of breakfast. Scrambling eggs, picking shells from the bowl, burning toast, zapping bacon. It is more circus than meal. When it is finally prepared, we sit and chat lazily about the important fact that we have nothing at all to do today.

I saunter out to the lawn and rummage around the small drainage canal that I have constructed to keep the rains from our basement. I trim a few hedges. Tidy up the garage. The rains have stopped now. Out of nowhere I ask my son if he cares to go for a bike ride. To my utter amazement he agrees. We have not gone on a bike ride together since he was eight. We laugh as we take turns jockeying for the lead.

Later that afternoon, we go to a movie together.

When we return, I head to the grocery store with my daughter. Mags will be gone to college in just a few weeks. I surprise her with some flowers that I bought along with the grocery sundries. She gives an "Oh, Dad!" and a peck on the cheek.

After we put the groceries away, I mosey outside to sit down on the porch steps and marvel at how pleasant this day of nothing has been.

Most days we seem obsessed with jamming as much activity into our lives as possible, especially on our days "off." Soccer matches, basketball tournaments, a gathering at the in-laws, a big game that must be watched on TV, community events, parties, concerts, shows, golf and biking, the constant social drone and buzz of the western world.

It seems that every day there is something we HAVE to do. And so few days to do simply what we WANT to do.

Like nothing.

I rediscovered something else this lazy weekend. Doing nothing is immensely relaxing.

Few conversations. No moments of panic when you can't remember where you are supposed to be next. No need to get appropriately dressed, for any garb is good for doing nothing.

And when I think about it, I am proud of all the things I got done this weekend while doing nothing.

I made breakfast for my kids.

I went on a bike ride with my son.

Bought flowers for my daughter.

Things I have been meaning to do but was too busy doing something instead of nothing.

Maybe it's when you are doing nothing at all that you get the most done.

I think I'll do nothing again next weekend.

12.04
SONGS OF A FATHER

All of this was accomplished with zero prodding or haranguing from the elders in the house. It just became his thing.

I am in the car with my son on the way to pick up a present for his seventeenth birthday. It is tiresome parental bragging, but the kid deserves something pretty good, as he is a pretty good kid. Solid student and athlete who has never really done much to embarrass or sadden his parents.

In fact, I am utterly sure I have embarrassed him far more often than he has me.

We pull into Ward-Brodt Music Mall along Todd Drive's commercial cluster of big boxes, and saunter inside to this hardware store for musicians. We make our way to a section where a regiment of guitars stands at attention. JT thinks this is all pretty cool.

In the last year, JT has developed a passion for and proficiency with the guitar, developed in the wake of an athletic injury that left him gimpy for much of his sophomore year. To work his way through the sadness of being sidelined, he quietly started plinking away at a cheap guitar we had bought him several years ago. Pretty soon the plinking started to sound like actual notes and chords. And then the chords began to sound like songs. All of this was accomplished with zero prodding or haranguing from the elders in the house. It just became his thing.

So, this year his birthday gift will be an effects gizmo for his guitar, further encouraging his newfound passion. Always looking to parent smartly, I did not want the gift — slightly pricey for a birthday present — to go without a droning life lesson from Dad. I tried to link the gizmo not only to the day he was born but also to his semester books and upcoming sports season.

"Son …" I intoned. "This is not just for your birthday, but for the good job you've done in school this year. Just keep hitting the books, and don't forget to work on that jump shot too."

And then, in one of those moments of change and clarity, JT turned to me, smiled and responded very calmly, "Dad, you don't have to tell me.

I know what I have to do." He said it matter-of-factly, without rancor. More like an FYI between two equals at work, rather than a father and son.

I nodded, "Well, JT … you just tell me when you want me to nudge you. OK?"

"Sure," he said. "I'll let you know." Then we both smiled and drove home to watch the Packers.

I would be happy if my era of parental nudging would end, as I have always struggled with how hard to push my kids in school and sports. Just how much encouragement is enough and how much is too much? How does a parent inspire and motivate without losing balance and rationality? How do you enable a child's interest yet still keep it fun? How do you keep sports in proper perspective, allowing them to complement, not overwhelm, scholastics, arts and personal integrity?

And then there is the most telling question … what is my motivation?

Do I want my kids to understand the nature of hard work and sacrifice for cohorts, lessons that will last long after the school games end? Sure.

Do I want them to achieve and realize the accorded benefits to those who do? Yup.

Do I want them to run around and collapse in fatigue with the belief that a tried adolescent is a good adolescent? You betcha.

But when does my desire for my son or daughters to achieve become more about me than them? More about my longing for them to live out my wishes for them, not their own dreams for themselves?

Or worse yet, do I long for my child to achieve so it might reflect well on me?

Ah, therein lies the rub.

The nature of kids' sports these days require a degree of commitment never experienced in previous generations. The regular season is barely over before the off-season leagues begin. Weekend after weekend of events created by adults, not kids. A volleyball tournament in Milwaukee. A basketball tournament in the Valley. A soccer trip to St. Louis. Hockey in Detroit. All of this so 14-year-olds can play the same game that their parents played in a park down the street, or a gym around the corner.

This is not at all bad. It is fun to travel with your adolescent, his buddies and their families. Clearly some of these trips are better form my son than sitting on his butt in front of the Xbox all weekend.

But it is not all good either. There is sometimes an unbalanced pressure; the sense of an imposed passion rather than one that springs naturally from the child. Coaches and parents barking and howling from the sidelines — clearly caring more about the games than the kids. There is the impact and cost of travel on home life. There are the tawdry sideline soap operas that come with team sports.

And so, a parent struggles with how much is enough and what is too much? When is it time to step away from the adrenaline and let your child determine and own what he or she wants to do?

My conversation with our youngest told me that perhaps my parental shift, at least on this front, might be winding down. A young man was applying my guidance to his own passion. One that will last him all his years. And that is why the father-son words in the car sounded so good.

Shortly after we got home, I heard another sound that was easy on my ears. Rising out of the basement I hear some sweet guitar. It was the sound of a kid, with prodding from no one but himself, working to get a little better.

And what a sweet song it is.

09.06
A RAINY DAY

It happened on that new patch of slick asphalt.

Rob Kozarek was doing everything a parent would want a son to do.
He was driving under the speed limit.
He was wearing a seat belt.
He was sober.
Typical Rob. Solid cat. Predictable, though, for a senior all-state footballer and honor roller thinking of playing for the Harvard Crimson next year.

Rob had just picked up his helmet and gear for an elite summer camp he was to attend prior to his final high school season. He was heading out on Highway 14 to the farm where he worked with a teammate, a halfback who enjoyed the privilege of running behind his massive frame.

But in a moment, an instant, Rob's life, and the plans he had, and the expectations his parents rightfully held, took a turn.

It happened on that new patch of slick asphalt. According to my Oregon friends, there have been problems for other drivers on that stretch in rain or snow. Makes a person wonder about the intellect of the road builders responsible for keeping our kids safe on a simple country road. How hard can that be?

Like several others that day, Rob's car hydroplaned in the rain. But Rob went down an embankment. Flipped more times than you care to envision. They showed the car in the paper the next day. Only someone with Rob's strength could have survived that mayhem.

The first we heard was that Rob was in critical condition with brain damage. There was a spontaneous prayer service that night. By then he was already upgraded to serious.

He was talking. He was still Rob. Bruised and swollen. But still Rob.

But he was also motionless from the waist down. Rob had fractured four cervical bones. His legs weren't working.

The news did not get much better in the ensuing days.

There was cause for hope that the spine had not been severed, but shocked.

Now Rob is at the Milwaukee Spine Institute, working to get better.

There is still that hope. But also the reality that it will be a long battle to regain motion in those powerful legs.

I visited Rob in the UW Hospital ICU a few days after the accident. It was one of those things that you want to do, but also dread, because you have to face a reality that you wish did not exist.

I talked briefly with Rob. I can't pretend that I knew him very well. To him, I was just another parent in the stands.

I also talked with the people I really went to visit: Rob's parents, John and Dar. I only knew them in passing, but I had a need to see them.

To tell them how devastated we were as a community. How hard we were praying. To assure them that they were not alone and that all sorts of folks were searching for ways to help.

And then, unplanned and out of nowhere, I found myself telling them a story about the last time I had been at the same hospital.

On that particular night, a smart hematology fellow was standing in the hospital hall outside my mother's room, telling me that she had the worst leukemia you can have. She had six to eight weeks to live.

I told the Kozareks that, at the same time, my son was dealing with a knee injury.

A far more minor thing than Rob was facing, but a trial nonetheless. He was told by more than one doc that he was done with high school sports.

I spoke of the anger I felt because I was so utterly powerless to help those I loved.

The Kozareks nodded. And then I tried to tell them about a moment that provided comfort in that time of utter despair.

The first came when I ran into a friend and Dominican nun, Sister Maggie Hopkins. She mentioned that I did not seem myself. I told her what was happening to the loved ones in my life. And here is what I cannot forget. And here is what I told John and Dar Kozarek.

Sister Maggie put her hand on my arm and said, with the confidence that only the strong in faith can convey, "John, your mom will be OK. And your son will be OK."

And then I suggested to the Kozareks that Rob would be OK.

And I told them one last story. It was the night of the prayer service. Folks were devastated by Rob's injury. I was leaving the church with my son, Rob's teammate.

I spoke of how sad it all was. JT stopped and put his arm on my shoulder and looked at me.

"Dad, you don't get it. We could be burying Rob. But now he's alive and getting better."

I nodded. JT continued, with that sense of hope that only the young possess.

"Dad, you don't really know Rob. I do. I played with him. You cannot believe how strong he is."

JT stopped a beat and then finished.

"He's going to be OK."

12.07
LAUGHING THROUGH CHRISTMAS

Hark the freakin' angels sing.

For a long time, when our children were young, I suffered through the Christmas blues.

The Irish are prone to melancholy, but the buoyant notion that each Christmas will be magic amplifies that Celtic tendency.

But somehow in the last few years I have found Christmas almost bearable.

Even funny.

Much of it has to do with my family, who now understand my struggle and work with me, like some sort of seasonal autistic.

Son JT has taken to helping me put up the Christmas lights. This ordeal had become so painful for me that I no longer placed the GE profit centers in the trees in front of our house, but simply wrapped them around the trunks. JT could tell that if this trend continued I would eventually run the extension cord to the curb and leave the lights in a jumbled ball in the gutter.

Thanks to my son, our lights are back in the tree limbs.

Hark the freakin' angels sing.

My wife has also been a big help. She understands that Christmas parties make me as uncomfortable as Mayor Dave at an Orchard Ridge neighborhood meeting. For that reason, Di has given me tacit permission to duck out of every party we attend shortly upon arrival.

My greatest moment on this front occurred several years ago. We entered a packed house full of beefy men in too-tight red wool vests. They actually looked downright dapper compared to the women in remarkably unattractive multicolored sweaters depicting everything from Santa and his reindeer landing on a roof to what I think was a space shuttle explosion.

I entered with bravado through the front door, worked my way through the house hugging all, telling them they looked wonderful, offering season's greetings, and then walked directly out the back door, around the side of the gaily lit house to my car.

Two hours later Diane called while I was watching a football game in my sweats and asked me how long I had stayed.

Told her I had just gotten home.

Another coping tactic has been to download obscure holiday songs off iTunes. Old R&B cuts and goofy celeb ditties make the holiday seem less strained. How can you not like Big Momma Thornton wailing "Silent Night" followed by Lorne Greene muttering his way through "Little Drummer Boy?" There is nothing better than musical kitsch to let us know just what lengths artists will go to to make money off the birth of the Christ child.

But mostly it has been our adult kids who have made the season fun.

First, in the same way someone checks to see if you have taken your meds, they demand that I sit and watch National Lampoon's *Christmas Vacation* starring Chevy Chase.

(This is back when he was funny).

The holiday antics of Clark Griswold and Cousin Eddie perfectly frame the absurd moments of Christmas and remind the overwhelmed viewer that things get nuts, crazy, maddening and frustrating for all. This film demands that you embrace your inner Clark. Once you've channeled Sparky's household, Christmas is a breeze.

After the Griswold gang has been viewed, even funnier tapes make their way into the machine and play throughout the holidays. They are the videos of our family Christmases Past.

The days when our children were actually children.

For hours on end on Christmas Eve and Christmas Day, our kids will watch the holiday moments that their harried parents captured with the video camera a decade and more ago.

There is Kate, the eldest, alternately rushing the camera and helping her younger siblings decorate cookies. There is the middle one, Maggie, who does her best to assert herself in the middle of the sibling hierarchy by constantly making sure that everyone knows which present is hers, thank you very much. And there is the youngest, JT, who executes one of the finest cookie-decorating maneuvers of all time using red sprinkles, M&Ms and his left nostril.

And that is how Christmas has become fun for this cynic. While reliving all those holidays that seemed so unpleasant, I hear, through the laughter of my children, that they were not that bad at all.

Indeed, to my surprise, that laughter makes me confront the notion that those Christmases might even have been wonderful.

Go figure.

Ho. Ho. Ho. Merry Christmas. Happy Hanukkah.

12.10
CANINE RECONSIDERED

My childhood experience with dogs—one dog actually—was consistently traumatic.

Not quite sure how this came about, but sometime in the last few months the two daughters/roommates in Chicago began talking about getting a dog.

Perhaps it was dissatisfaction with men their age. Or the unrelenting call of estrogen that makes young women want to mother something. Anything.

Either way, "getting a dog" became a persistent point of conversation during our long-distance FaceTime calls, or when Kate and Mags hustled up I-90 for a Badger game and lolled about Sunday morn over coffee before the drive back.

They approached me with temerity on the subject. Understandable, as I have reputation of being The Anti-Dog Dad.

There is truth to this charge. My childhood experience with dogs, one dog actually, was consistently traumatic. The mutt's name was Candy, an orphan that Mom and Dad got for us while we were living on Norwood Place in the sixties. A mid-sized cross between spaniel and retriever, she was likable enough.

But dropping an untrained dog into a household of six Irish Catholic kids, all seemingly born nine months and one week apart, was a wild example of taking human chaos and then adding animal chaos on top of it. We had no idea how to train or care for Candy.

Every day we would tie her up in the backyard with cheap, rubber-coated laundry line and every day she would break said line and chase the Illinois Central train down the tracks as it left town. All of us would weep and sob, knowing that Candy had been run over by a succession of coal cars, only to rejoice when she returned an hour later exhausted by the ten-mile run, and frustrated that she had not been able to wrestle the train to the ground.

This went on for months, until Mom and Dad took Candy to "a nice couple on a farm." I still can't ask my dad what they actually did with her.

The ensuing years did not make me care for dogs more. My tolerance for crotch sniffing, lawn befouling and unleashed rushes at me while jogging or biking conspired to make me a dog curmudgeon. My favorite quote to dog-loving friends was always, "Yeah, right — 'He's a nice dog, he won't bite' are the last words everyone hears before they head to the emergency room for stitches."

I steadfastly opposed getting a dog while our children were younger. A break from the unrelenting task of changing diapers by walking around the neighborhood carrying a plastic bag full of dog waste isn't the quiet time a harried young dad needs.

And how can anyone hope to carry on a neighborly conversation while blithely pretending you're not carrying a warm wad of dog feces wrapped in a Copp's bag in your right hand? Seriously. How can anyone do that?

We had a mouse once. My kids still remind me of their trauma when he died of overeating and I unceremoniously threw him into the woods off our deck. So a dog seemed utterly out of the question.

But then I met Ozzie.

Ozzie was the companion of Steve, one of our kids' closest friends, and the only canine ever welcome at the Roach cabin. Indeed, he became a mascot. His quiet, mature friendliness and intelligence was a revelation to me. I christened Ozzie "The Only Dog I Ever Liked." I still remember our eldest Kate calling to inform me, with a tear in her voice, that Ozzie had passed.

So it was with great trepidation, but an open mind, that I greeted Philly, when daughter Mags brought him home the first time this fall. A fox-like mix of Collie and retriever, Philly was rescued by our girls from a Chicago shelter.

Maggie asked if I would watch Philly while she headed down to the game to party with all the recent Badger grads. I agreed.

And to my surprise, I was smitten.

Philly was a blast to walk, every squirrel a revelation, every bird a discovery. He quickened my usual pace by straining at the leash, not because he is rude, but because he thought the park behind our house was the Most Beautiful Spectacular Thing he had ever seen.

He made me view it, and other things in my world, in new light. I was stunned by the simple pleasure I took in his quiet company as I read on the back deck while he lounged at my feet. I even began to think that he liked me.

My reaction to this animal has been, frankly, stunning.

And now, I am embarrassed to admit, I can't wait for the girls to bring him home for the holidays.

I am so taken by Philly that I am thinking of buying him a freakin' Christmas present.

All of this has made me wonder.

Have dogs changed all that much?

12.11
THE YEAR OF THE DOG

Sure, he was hyper and manic, but he was also smart. And interesting.

The guy from MG&E came by this week. He sprayed neon orange paint on our lawn, all the way from the front curb to the back deck, revealing where the electric cables lurk. He was able to navigate the area despite the fierce protective instincts of our new pooch, Phillip Seymour Dog.

Phil has been with us a year. His story is remarkable for several reasons, the least being that his new owner has historically viewed dogs with abhorrence.

Phil was left at our house in November of last year via our daughters, now living and working in Chicago. A combination of estrogen and lifelong wish fulfillment had compelled them to go to an animal shelter and select Phil from a sad array of urban strays who were mere hours from euthanasia. Although Kate and Mags always wanted a dog, they were denied that privilege in their youth, as their younger brother was allergic to critters and their Pops was a curmudgeon regarding pets.

Our kids did once have a white mouse. He died of obesity in a cage in our laundry room. Our children are still appalled at the funeral he received. The ceremony? I put on a glove, carried him out the back door and threw him into the woods off our deck.

Hey, he was too big to flush.

This very back page has been used to chronicle the issues Dad has had with dogs, including their penchant for sniffing crotches and soiling the yard. Behavior we would not tolerate from humans. Canines also play a lead role in the eternal drama of speeding to the emergency room after hearing the words, "Don't worry. He won't bite."

Phil first visited our home last Thanksgiving. The daughters were weary after a frantic ride from Chicago with the collie/husky/cattle dog/shepherd/Tasmanian Devil mix flying around the car for three hours straight. Thanks to their upbringing, the girls had absolutely no idea how to handle the thing. Not only were the daughters exhausted, but they were also understandably anxious about their dad's reaction to the mutt. They knew it wasn't going to be good.

But to their surprise, and mine, I discovered, after an afternoon reading on the back porch with Phil, that I kinda liked the guy.

Sure, he was hyper and manic, but he was also smart. And interesting.

But sadly, Phil was too much to handle in Chicago. Long work hours and a small condo are no formula for dog serenity. The girls were teary at the thought of returning him to the shelter. So, much to everyone's amazement and the wife's chagrin, I suggested that he stay with us on a short-term contract. I viewed myself as the Hero Dad, taking one for the team.

The first several weeks with Phil were horrific. He was wary of us and we knew absolutely nothing about the animal and how to control him. In his anxiety with our ignorance, he chewed leather car upholstery, lawn chairs, exercise equipment and our digits. After nine long dog days we decided that we had to return Phil to a shelter. He was simply too much. After all, we had just finished raising three large mammals of our own. We deserved a break.

The next morning, after a restless sleep, I called the shelter and made arrangements. We would have one more day with Phil. I slept little that final night, shocked at the emotion I was feeling about thirty pounds of frenetic mutt. In the morning, after three bracing cups of coffee, I confessed to Diane that I did not want to part with Phillip Seymour Dog. Diane was understanding, but disappointed. She liked the thing, but he was driving her nuts. I promised to fully own the project, with the qualification that this was simply a one-month extension, not a long-term contract.

Phil was on probation. A short leash, if you will.

Through the spring and summer Phil and I got to know each other. I discovered the Zen of dog walking. He learned to chill. We have reached a good point in our relationship. I feed him and he, in turn, acts happy to see me. This is a new experience. Humans are often interested to see me, but rarely jump up and down giddy and happy upon my arrival.

Phil, on the other hand, does this every single time I walk up to him. How can this not be good for the soul?

The orange paint on the lawn is dry. This week the fence guys come to build a dog run off our deck. Phil will have a penthouse from which to monitor the squirrels and keep his master safe.

And our family will enjoy a traditional holiday gift with a twist.

Our kids will not get a puppy for Christmas.

But they will get to keep one.

05.15
MARY'S PRAYER

"There is something wrong with Mary."

I first met Mary Ripple in 1967. We were freshmen in high school. Like all freshmen, we were confused and anxious, thrown into a new world. Yet Mary was quick with a laugh and naturally friendly.

That following summer, back when the sun and water were not a threat, I ran into her at Vilas Beach. She was with her sister Diane, who was a year younger and shy. For whatever reason, I was immediately and forever attracted to Diane.

The years moved forward and Mary's sister, the skinny girl in the polka-dot bikini, became my wife, and Mary became my sister-in-law. During our courtship, Diane and I set up Mary with my roommate and coaching buddy, John Boyle, and to our surprise they got married before we did.

Mary and Diane, always the closest of sisters, were nicknamed Brenda and Cobina, after a female comedy duo who starred opposite the Three Stooges, by their parents, Don and Mary Anne. They got that moniker right.

As the years advanced, the two sisters began to have kids, all in a cluster. For all practical purposes, Mary and Diane raised their six children as siblings.

John Boyle went on to become one of the more successful basketball coaches in the Madison area, taking both the East Purgolders and the Middleton Cardinals to the state championship finals. Sons Danny and Tone were fine local high school players. Mary was at every game, supporting everyone, every step of the way.

As time passed, and Diane and Mary kicked their kids out into the world, they were able to spend more time together as sisters, less burdened by motherhood. Although when they would get together, they'd share worry about their kids, as good moms do forever.

It was on a Florida getaway with just the two sisters when Diane, a nurse, became concerned. The night she arrived home, we sat down at the kitchen table and Diane said starkly, "There is something wrong with Mary." On their vacation, Mary was strangely confused, constantly losing her purse and talking to herself as she obsessively cleaned the condo.

It turns out that Diane was right. There was something wrong. After months of angst and tests, it was determined that Mary had Alzheimer's disease. She was 57 years old when she was diagnosed. Fifty. Seven.

John retired from teaching shortly thereafter. Mary's oldest child, Haley, quit a thriving career that had taken her to New York, Los Angeles and Chicago and moved back to Middleton. John, Haley and Diane soon became Mary's primary caregivers, with the rest of the clan doing what we could when we could.

At first Mary's disease was manageable. Though she couldn't access your name, or the right words to express the beauty of a tree, she was, in very many ways, still Mary. She was masterful at pretending she could remember someone as she gave them a hug. Strangely, one aspect of her disease created moments when it was as if she were seeing a sunset or a full moon for the very first time. Mary's reborn appreciation for the beauty of the natural world that her brain had somehow forgotten was a reminder and sad gift to all of us.

Now, five years since her diagnosis, we see only brief flashes of the woman we all loved. The demands made on the care team are relentless. Each day brings uncertainty and some other new, brutal reality.

Our two families' clan, never a quiet group, is not taking Mary's battle with Alzheimer's passively. Two years ago, in an effort to do something, anything, to battle Mary's disease, Haley organized an event called Blondes vs. Brunettes, a flag football game featuring young women raising money to support Alzheimer's research. They throw themselves around the football field with abandon, fighting each other in good sport as they fight the disease that has stolen Mary and so many of their family members.

This year, on May 3 at one o'clock, the girls will kick off again. They will be decked out in all their glory. The anthem will be sung. And the color commentary from the booth at Keva Sports Center in Middleton will be provided by the always funny James Roach, along with this writer as his sidekick. The Roach daughters, Kate and Mags, will make their way from Chicago to stand alongside their blonde cousin/sister Haley, prepared to wreak havoc on the Brunettes.

Although Mary's condition has worsened, she may be able to attend the game. But her behavior is altered. For a woman who was everyone's greatest cheerleader, it is a tough, sad thing to witness how her cheers have died.

But on that day, it will be our prayer that Mary, who cheered on so many others for so long, might somehow, somewhere in the compromised biology of her brain, know that it is now all of us who cheer desperately for her.

05.18
THE BASEBALL GLOVE

....

What happened next was heard by the pitcher, catcher, umpire and folks in the stands. It was a sound that some would remember for years.

The location was Breese Stevens Field.

The event was the Madison City League Baseball Championship.

The time was the summer of 1966.

The players on the field were 13 years old, with the west-side Madison team playing the east-side Madison team for the city title.

There was a good crowd in the stands. Youth City League baseball was a popular neighborhood affair and had yet to be eclipsed by the more formal Little League experience. In a smaller Madison in those days, it was a big game. The *Wisconsin State Journal* and the *Capital Times* would cover it, photos included.

In the middle innings, a kid from the west side slapped a banjo single into right center, then stole second and reached third on a passed ball.

The stage was set for a little drama.

The east-side pitcher, a talented athlete named Johnny Czerepinski, delivered. The batter hit a grounder to the second baseman. The kid on third sped toward home with the leading run. Rather than take the easy play at first, the second baseman threw to home to the catcher.

What happened next was heard by the pitcher, catcher, umpire and folks in the stands. It was a sound that some would remember for years.

The runner on third, while sliding into home base, caught his spike on the perimeter of the embedded rubber structure that constituted home plate at Breese Stevens. The runner, who was called safe, kept sliding forward while his leg stopped. Something had to give and that something was the runner's tibia and fibula. They broke with a snap.

The game came to a halt. The next several minutes were composed of a bevy of folks attending to the runner who lay on home base in pain and bewilderment. In a sign that is never good, the kid's father was called down from the stands. As this was the pre-cell phone era, someone scurried inside of the bowels of Breese Stevens to make a call for help. Soon, the boy and his father were bundled into an ambulance and carried off to St. Mary's Hospital.

Despite Czerepinski's stellar performance, the west siders ended up winning the game.

Two days after the incident, and still in the hospital, the injured ballplayer received a card from Johnny Czerepinski expressing his heartfelt wishes for a quick recovery. It was a remarkably classy act for a 13-year-old, one the kid with the broken leg would remember.

Fifty-two years later, Czerepinski admitted that the card was his idea, though he got help from his parents finding an address.

The card so impressed the father of the injured ballplayer that he sent Johnny Czerepinski a gift certificate to his place of business on State Street.

The business was called Badger Sporting Goods. The gift certificate was for $25, an astronomical amount in those days. Young Czerepinski, who played with a used baseball glove because he could never afford a new one, was able to buy the best baseball glove in the store, and a new bat to boot. Czerepinski would use the glove he got that day at Badger Sporting Goods for the next 25 years.

Breese Stevens Field is no longer a baseball field. It's currently used for soccer, food festivals and REO Speedwagon concerts.

Czerepinski still lives on Madison's east side.

The kid who didn't know how to slide is this columnist.

And it was John James Roach, my father, who sent Johnny Czerepinski the gift certificate for that brand-new leather baseball glove.

Dad passed away on Feb. 24 of this year at the age of 88.

He never mentioned what he did for Czerepinski. I learned of it by happenstance a half-century later from Johnny.

Nor was Dad inclined to speak of the countless other generous things he did for young athletes, coaches and friends alike.

If you ask around town, most folks will tell you, that was the man he was.

08.18
DOG GONE

Despite all the mayhem, we had bonded in the way only a human can connect with a dog.

The entire gang recently gathered at the lake. Three of them weren't human.

We were also joined by Lucy, Finley and Pork Chop—two Labs and a bulldog.

The canine pals added endless entertainment and comfort to our summer vacation.

There was one dog that wasn't there: our own pooch, Phillip Seymour Dog, aka Philly.

Philly, a border collie shepherd mix, joined our family nearly eight years ago, rescued from a Chicago kennel only days before he was to be euthanized. His adoption was the idea of our two daughters, Kate and Maggie, who lived together at the time. They thought Philly would be a good break from the pressure of their work. They had always wanted a dog.

But it quickly became clear that Phil was not a condo dog. He needed to run. Constantly. It became such an issue that our girls would become teary discussing the prospect of returning him to the rescue shelter because he had been returned several times already. Another unhappy owner would bring him to an awful fate.

So, on impulse, I said I'd take Phil. I'd met him and liked him. And he seemed to like me, not always an easy thing for other creatures of the planet.

The first night with Phil was disastrous. He was anxious and hyper. I nearly fell down the stairs in the dark trying to get to him and quiet him down.

The next morning, we called to make arrangements to take him to yet another shelter, this time in Madison. I didn't sleep that second night. Despite all the mayhem, we had bonded in the way only a human can connect with a dog. Sometime around 3 a.m., I decided I couldn't let Phil go.

And so, for the next five years Phil was my companion. We walked in the morning and evening, where I learned that dog walking is a form of meditation. It forces you out into the natural world during all seasons. And while your dog sniffs about, you ponder the things that need pondering.

Phil was also instrumental in changing me. Instead of stopping at the tavern, I'd come home to walk him. Always the better choice. In the evenings, instead of slumping in front of the television set, I'd sit outside on the porch and read while endlessly tossing the ball to my pal.

It took Phil time to warm to me. I am sure his previous Chicago owners beat him. He would let me pet him, but he wouldn't settle down next to me. Then one night, about three months into our relationship, Madison was hit by a thunderstorm. A frightened and shaking Phil came and sat on my lap for the very first time, and I comforted him. It was a memorable moment in our relationship; an acknowledgement by Phil that I was a human who wouldn't hurt him.

Phil was a smart, fun dog.

But he had issues. He once rushed our neighbor when he managed to get off-leash. He traveled poorly and tore up the back seat of our car. And as he became more comfortable at our home, he became more territorial. If you invaded areas he perceived to be his own, he would growl and become a different Phil. Because I was a neophyte dog owner, I didn't know what to do. We tried dog trainers. It helped, but never changed Phil completely.

And then came the time when we decided we couldn't care of Phil any longer. Three, then four human family members began requiring their own care. Serious care. A demanding animal became too demanding.

So, we surrendered Phil to a great rescue place called Fetch. I shed tears. He was such a good companion. In whatever mystical way dogs and humans connect, we did. Phil gave me a greater appreciation of other living creatures, as beautiful a gift as any you can receive.

I'm not sure what became of Phil, but I think about him often. I hope he knows how much I cared for him, and that I did my best. And that I'm sorry. Even though we gave him a great five years, yet another family had to give him up.

The whole thing makes me terribly sad in the way only a dog who has gone away can.

Every time the thunder sounds, I think of him.

THE NEW PARIS

There are lots of towns that have lakes, and yet they succeed in being tremendously boring. I post that it is our isthmus that makes us so interesting. We have managed to pack a riot of neighborhoods, a huge university, forty thousand adolescents, two thousand beret-wearing professors, a state capitol, a couple hundred beefy, drunk legislators and lobbyists, a squad of goofy aldermen and nine gyro restaurants into approximately three square blocks.

09.03
I AM PEDESTRIAN,
HEAR ME ROAR

I met with my parents and announced to them that I am pedestrian myself. They took the news as graciously as one could expect.

I am driving to work on the street in the neighborhood I grew up in on Madison's West Side. Just as I near Michael's Frozen Custard and Wingra Park, I spy a gaggle of folks walking stridently across Monroe Street waving red plastic flags attached to white plastic sticks in the faces of idling commuters.

Madison has long been a hot bed of political activism. The peace movement. Women's rights. Black rights. Gay rights.

Now we are a hot bed for another cause. Pedestrian rights. Red flags, yard signs, billboards and speed bumps are flourishing all around Madison, bravely touting and protecting the right to cross the street safely.

I met with my parents and announced to them that I am pedestrian myself. They took the news as graciously as one could expect.

As a practicing pedestrian, I totally support not being hit by cars. Indeed, I have tragically lost a family relative in such a way. But at the same time, I cannot help but think that all this flag waving is, well, a little … goofy.

This is a daring thing to admit, as it is unpopular to be against pedestrian safety, just as it is hard to be for drunk driving.

But here is the problem. First, I feel like these pedestrianistas are somehow angry at me for driving to work. This is not wholly fair, as I never held a gun to their head to make them move along Monroe Street, which was a busy road long before they were born or hit town. I am also not the one who developed much of the Land Beyond the Beltline, which has contributed to traffic bedlam on all of Madison's major arterials.

I also worry that a few of these well-intentioned folks might naively believe that a red plastic flag will somehow be enough to stop a car driven by a coffee-swilling, cellphone-talking commuter in an SUV.

It won't. When it comes to Pedestrian versus Car, the auto has historically dominated.

I do not think that the addition of a red plastic flag will alter this outcome markedly.

And there is another question. Has anyone ever been killed crossing Monroe Street?

I was with six folks my age, who have spent over four decades each — a collective total of 240 years — crossing Monroe Street, and we had no memory of anyone being killed crossing the aforesaid thoroughfare.

Nonetheless, these pedestrian rightists are well-intentioned. But I would like to be so bold as to suggest another use for their waving red flags and erstwhile grass roots organizational energies.

I would like it if they waved their red flags in the faces of the city traffic managers and planners.

And while they are at it, I would like it if they waved their red flags in the faces of the real estate speculators and alder people who have allowed much of Monroe Street, and other older Madison neighborhoods flush with empty store fronts, to resemble downtown Gary.

They could even wave their red flags in the faces of whomever is in charge of making sure Dane County doesn't have a murder every damn day.

This might be a better use of local political energy rather than guilting folks who are just trying to get to work in the morning.

And if they continue having pedestrian problems they could just talk to my mom, who issued a warning to me 40 years ago.

"Johnny, be very careful crossing the street."

And she wasn't even waving a red flag in my face.

12.03
~~EAT~~ *Thank* THE RICH

The names are listed along the ceiling like stars in the firmament.

It is a difficult day when a loved one is admitted to hospice. Dad and the exhausted sisters had already made their way home.

We tried to make sure that Mom was comfortable, as comfortable as you can be with death hovering. We whispered that we loved her and bade good night to my younger brothers, who were settling down to spend the darker, lonely hours in Mom's spacious room.

She would sleep much of the night. Dan and Jimmy would watch Mom … and the Cubs.

Wife Diane and other brother Bobby and I stopped for a drink and dinner before heading home. It gave us a chance to digest not only a bit of food, but also the reality we were encountering.

And that's when we ran into Fred and Gary.

Fred Schwartz is an old Blessed Sacrament grade school chum. Good basketball player who now has the knees to prove it. He married another friend, high school classmate Debbie Bakke of the Sub-Zero Bakkes, who have been making fine ways to keep things cool for many years here in Madison. Her brother now runs the shop that his late father started.

Gary is Gary Steinhauer of the Madison family known for both fine golf swings and fine butter.

It was fortuitous that I bumped into these guys. I asked them to join us for a beer.

I wanted to thank them.

When you walk into the entrance of the Bill and Marilyn Anderson Hospice Center, tucked into a beautiful oak savannah down a quiet road in Fitchburg, you see a tasteful reminder of the Madison families, along with the Andersons, who have helped create the building and the experience.

The names are listed along the ceiling like stars in the firmament.

They are names known to most anyone who has grown up in Madison. Aside from building successful family businesses that employ thousands of Madisonians, they are also the folks most everyone calls when they need help for a school, a children's hospital, a cancer ward or a hospice center.

Flesch, Wall, Krantz, Endres, Bakke and Steinhauer — and the short list of other Madison names — come up on every Palm Pilot of every fundraiser in town, right after the Frautschis.

It's to the point where you want to yell, "Hey, could someone else in town possibly make a few million bucks here to take the load off these guys?"

Of course, when asked, they don't have to give a damn cent. But when the call comes, these families often respond in the same way.

They say, "Yes."

So, when I sat down with Fred and Gary, I told them of Mom's condition and her new, sadly temporary quarters. And then I thanked them personally for the profound help their kindness provided Mom and our family.

Both Fred and Gary huffed and deflected the gratitude. They said it was all about the standard set by the fathers and mothers who built the companies. You hear the same thing from the other successful clans in town.

Seems that aside from business savvy and an impressive work ethic, goodness is also a family trait.

Madison is not a big city. These same families always get that first call to support our community's charitable efforts to the point that it seems that they are taken for granted.

What a mistake. They aren't.

Here is what I told Fred and Gary on behalf of my family. It's also what I say to all the rest of those names that I have not chronicled in the hospice firmament, as well as the names on every wall, ceiling, sculpture or plaque for every charitably funded building and program in town.

Tell your dads or moms or in-laws or brothers or whoever that their simple, quiet generosity, that brief hand stroke on that check, has had a profound effect on our family in a time of near-desperate need.

Tell them that for all the refrigerators, pounds of butter, tons of meat, machine parts, dolls, wieners, printed brochures, copying machines or school supplies your family produces and sells, none of it compares to the impact that your fortunes have had on our family during its saddest hour.

Tell them we don't take it for granted.

Tell them it won't be forgotten.

Tell those names in the firmament thanks.

Thanks so much.

03.06
WHEN ART GOES BAD

....

When I first saw this oversized ode to bat guano, I was aghast.

Now that the football has ended and we are free of the usual distractions that accompany every season, it is time to turn our attention to the venereal piece of concrete someone stuck at the west gateway to the University of Wisconsin campus. It stands in front of Camp Randall and offers us the one finger salute every day.

I am referring, of course, to the odd stack of fossilized footballs cutely dubbed "Nails Tails."

This sterling example of public art gone bad was erected (pardon the verb) late last fall, after several months of flawed work by the sculptor and UW grad Donald Lipski.

When I first saw this oversized ode to bat guano, I was aghast. I am sure that Mr. Lipski has done some wonderful sculptures in the past. This isn't one of them.

How could anyone approve such a poor artistic effort? How could anyone choose to honor a program and place that has done so many things right by commissioning something that offers stunning testimony of how to do things dreadfully wrong?

At first, I surmised that it was the work of the Athletic Department. Perhaps they chose to make the piece just as awful as it could be as retribution for being forced to pay for public art as part of the Camp Randall renovations. I was ready to accuse the jock execs inside Camp Randall of being Anti-Art.

Or, to put a finer point on it, anti-community.

The quaint and predictable retort of bad artists is to claim that much esteemed art was once deemed controversial. This is the use of cheap condescension to dodge responsibility.

As someone who makes his living in the arts and who has done more than his fair share of substandard work, I am here to tell you that anyone who claims "Nails Tails" to be controversial is delusional.

There is nothing remotely controversial about "Nails Tails." It is not good enough to engender controversy.

I have yet to hear a single soul defend its artistic statement in a way that would remotely resemble a controversy.

In fact, there may be near unanimity that it is bad art. And we are stuck with some.

Lest you question the discriminating act of declaring something bad art, please consider the fact that some works of art are considered great. To me, those examples are the proof that a lot of art does not come close.

There are books that need more editing. Films that never should have been made. Actors who are hammy. Concerts that were sloppy. Portraits with poor perspective. And magazine columns that are ill conceived.

There also are sculptures that are poorly envisioned and cast. "Nails Tails" falls, with a resounding thud, into this category.

And, with respect, here is why I think Mr. Lipski missed the boat.

He viewed the stadium with a shallow, simplistic, even condescending view. The public space that is Camp Randall on an autumn Saturday is really not about football at all. It is about community. It is color, brass bands and friends reunited. It is a celebration, not of football, but of one of the greatest learning communities in the world.

But what did we get to symbolize this experience? An inside joke.

Mr. Lipski has stated that his work is a bit of an ode to his former college roommate. Aside from the fact that Freud would have a field day with the artistic statement that resulted from that friendship, it does allow one to pose this question to Mr. Lipski: If this sculpture is about your roommate, is it not private rather than public art?

But let's be honest. Mr. Lipski is not the culprit. The Wisconsin Art Board and chair Lieutenant Gov. Barbara Lawton are truly at fault. They erred either by hiring the wrong artist for the job or for failing to give Mr. Lipski proper direction on his quarter-million-dollar project.

And now what should they do? Easy answer.

They should do what Ron Wolf did with Ray Rhodes. What the Coca-Cola Company did with New Coke. What Dustin Hoffman and Warren Beatty did after Ishtar.

Admit that it was all a terrible mistake.

Lieutenant Gov. Lawton and Gov. Jim Doyle (who grew up in the neighborhood and should have done better by his homies) should also commission another work.

A work of art that folks can embrace as a symbol of community and shared experience.

WHILE I HAVE YOUR ATTENTION

A work of art that families will pose beside for pictures.

A work of art that the networks will feature as they open their broadcasts.

A work of good, even heroic, art that lovers will visit on their honeymoon and speak of the day they fell for each other while watching the Badgers in Madtown.

This still leaves us with one final question.

What do we do with the priapistic pile of pigskin that mars the corner of Regent and Monroe?

My suggestion? Simple.

Use it to shore up the bridge on Seminole Highway.

04.06
THE NEW PARIS

[W]hen was the last time someone went to Nebraska for Halloween?

Gauging by the contents of the rest of the magazine, I gather we are celebrating Madison's 150th birthday.

The old gal looks pretty good.

As a homie, I would like to offer up three things that I think separate our fair burg from America's gaggle of dowdy towns.

First, our lakes.

To be a truly great city, you need water.

San Frank, New York and Chicago all have water. Los Angeles has water, too, but somehow it has managed to become an awful city despite the Pacific Ocean.

Most midwestern towns don't have much water, and so they are deemed boring.

Not Madison. You can't take a wrong turn in this town without plunging your car into a lake. In fact, it is a regular act for our cops to pull the occasional Dodge up the shoreline as the result of some poor mope making a bad bar-time turn.

But there is also a sad, ugly side to our waters that the *New York Times* never mentions when they wax eloquently about our lakes.

They stink. Smell to high heaven several months out of the year.

In fact, the only time they don't reek is when they are frozen solid.

If we want to gauge how great a city we truly are, we should work hard to improve the state of our lakes. Then, ten years from now, we can sniff the air in August. If it smells like fresh, clean water rather than dead fish, stranded ducks and rotting water weeds, we can assume have cleaned our soiled nest and can lay honest claim to our accolades.

The second thing that sets us apart from other midwestern habitats is that our ancestors, after they shoved the resident Native Americans aside, chose to inhabit, of all things, an isthmus.

Jared Diamond, a UCLA geography professor-cum-philosopher, has turned heads lately by stating the well-considered obvious: that human cultures are shaped most by the land they inhabit. There are lots of towns that have lakes, and yet they succeed in being tremendously boring. I posit that it is our isthmus that makes us interesting.

We have managed to pack a riot of neighborhoods; a huge university; forty thousand adolescents; two thousand beret-wearing professors; a state capitol; a couple hundred beefy, drunk legislators and lobbyists; a squad of goofy aldermen and nine gyro restaurants into approximately three square blocks.

And all of them love to debate.

And all of them think that they alone are right.

No wonder we are interesting.

Our isthmus serves as a hothouse of ideas and personalities. If we had dispersed all this cultural and political bounty over a couple hundred square miles instead of State Street, we'd be Lincoln, Nebraska.

And when was the last time someone went to Nebraska for Halloween?

The third reason we are interesting is the most important.

It is the University of Wisconsin-Madison.

The University has made our little town intellectually and culturally diverse in a way few small cities could ever hope to be. The University allows us to enjoy a stunning array of concerts, speeches, political rallies and athletic events that often draw the attention of the nation.

The University keeps us wonderfully young, with an influx of fresh brains every fall.

The University means that you can bump into a giant of stem cell research and a frontrunner for a Nobel at your local coffee shop.

Truth is, the University of Wisconsin is what makes Madison both different and important.

It makes for a place where you can sip a Terrace beer on a summer's eve, and as the sun sets over Mendota, hear folks at the tables near you converse in four different languages.

As a Chicago buddy once remarked to me on his first summer visit to the Terrace, "Geez. This feels like Paris."

Yes, if we are honest with ourselves, it is the UW that makes us more special and has for 150 years.

It makes a homie wonder what kind of city we would be without it.

My answer?

Sheboygan.

10.10
JACKET AND TIE

And you wanted to believe in the story, if for no other reason than someone was finally trying something different.

Last year, while wandering around the web, I came across a stirring video.

It told the tale of the graduating class of Englewood Prep in Chicago. The story wasn't just that all 107 graduating seniors had received college acceptance letters.

No, what caught my eye, and moved me damn near to tears was that all 107 members of the Englewood Prep class were young, black and male. These were boys who came from difficult circumstances and tough neighborhoods. Few people, if any, had lofty expectations for them.

But now here they were, celebrating their college acceptance letters. The video showed them in the gym bleachers, dressed in jackets and ties, standing and applauding each other as their astounding achievement was announced.

Their shared pride was powerful to see. And you wanted to believe in the story, if for no other reason than someone was finally trying something different.

And now there is the chance for such a story to be told in Madison. According to a recent *Capital Times* piece by Susan Troller, the president of the Urban League of Greater Madison, Kaleem Caire, has a vision. Caire, a Madison West alum, is working to create a school for Madison-area boys of color only, covering grades six through twelve. The school would have a strict academic regimen for the boys in their most formative years.

The *Cap Times*'s online message board was alive with comments, as any story alluding to race in America is sure to provoke. But it is hard to see anything bad about considering this progressive move when the stark statistics about young black American males are examined.

Go to Google. Regardless of political bias, the state of young black men in our country must be seen as a condition of chronic societal problems with few transformational solutions.

Look at unemployment stats. Testing and college data. Prison enrollment. Drug use and violent crime reports. Fatherless household numbers. The litany is shattering.

It is not an illogical leap to state that the social health of young black males is our nation's single greatest domestic issue, with costs and pain that ripple across all of our lives.

It is the problem that we, America, can't solve.

The explanations for this situation are abundant and controversial. But whether a citizen views the core issue as white racism, bureaucratic bungling and waste, or collective parental irresponsibility in poorer black communities, the one thing most everyone can agree on is that there is a problem.

And over the last few decades this problem has arrived in Madison. We now have a fixed underclass, suffering from issues our local systems still struggle to understand and confront. These problems manifest themselves every single day in Madison schools, buses, neighborhoods and emergency rooms, with teachers, cops and hospital staff manning the front lines where poverty and ignorance combine to create chaos.

We also see it in the quiet migration few speak of in Madison; the white flight to suburban communities that surround our city. Outside the city, school enrollments are still overwhelmingly white, while populations of color in the county have increased.

Further compounding the problem is that we still seem to lack language to speak honestly of the issues. White folks seem skittish, defensive and fearful of using the wrong word. And black Madisonians share frustration and anger, often struggling to be understood.

And so we, all of us, end up with lost children.

But there are signs of hope. And solutions. Best of all they are coming, almost spontaneously, from black communities around America. Geoffrey Canada of the Harlem's Children Zone has created a national sensation with his revolutionary teaching and educational community creation involving both students and parents. Others now argue, not unlike Caire, that a return to a sort of enlightened segregation, derivative of America's black colleges, may be a solution.

That is why the Englewood grads and Kaleem Caire's proposal was so intriguing. They offer emergent black solutions to problems that the nation has not come close to solving for decades. Imagine a society where whole populations of young people are viewed not as a liability but and asset? How could there not be benefit and savings for all?

Of course, there will opposition to this educational alternative in Madison. There always is.

But here is a response to those objections.

Ask folks to take a look at the cost and productivity of the Chicago, Detroit or Milwaukee public school systems and ask one thing: Got any better ideas?

01.11
WHEN THE WALL CAME TUMBLING

As it turns out, the wall was a Badger football fan. Who isn't?

The large wall had stood for decades, holding silent watch over the events of the Vilas neighborhood. Its tons of heavy bricks, stacked more than 10 feet high, overlooked the zoo. It had heard elephants trumpet.

Lions roar. Peacocks call. But rain, ice and snow had worked inexorably to weaken its base.

No one knew, least of all the two young boys tossing a football in its shadow, that it was desperately holding fast for just a few more minutes until the boys were done with their game.

If it managed to stay upright for a bit longer, history might smile on us all.

As it turns out, the wall was a Badger football fan. Who isn't?

It has been a great year for Bucky. The team is one of the finest in the land. Perhaps the best Badger football assemblage to ever take the field. They have a stunningly smart and accurate quarterback, a tight end worthy of Pat Richter's position, a bevy of running backs, each better than the next. And before them, an offensive line that moves like some great glacier: large, mostly white and overwhelming. And finally, a defensive end who plays like there is a Bunyan in the family's lineage.

Soon they will compete for the Big Bouquet.

But what makes this Badger team great is not just the players. Now they have a head coach as good as they are. As the Badgers slapped Ohio State, it was clear that we were watching not just a senior class, but also a head coach, come of age.

Bret Bielema, whose challenging fate was to learn on the job, had finally bested a ranked team, not only asserting himself as the coach Barry Alvarez expected him to be, but as the leader the players and community required.

Bielema's development, after an uneven start, has been satisfying to watch. And cause for new respect motivated by factors beyond the simple winning of college football games.

It is also another victory for Barry, whose swagger now carries wisdom as well.

But for locals there is another man for whom we celebrate. His dad coached us. His mom taught us. His brothers and sisters are our friends. During the final quarter of the Ohio State game, as the Badgers began their game-winning drive deep in their own territory by throwing five passes IN A ROW!!!, I texted Rick, Paul Chryst's older brother, the words, "Somewhere George is smiling."

George Chryst was Paul's late father. He grew up in Madison. Played for Edgewood and the Badgers and returned to coach at both schools. He was known to run the occasional audacious play.

Surely the Badger success can be credited to his son, Paul, as well as Bret Bielema. Indeed, it would not be unfair to refer to the humble Heimer (his family and neighborhood nickname) by the term Assistant Head Coach.

It is not a stretch to claim that the emotional leadership and energy of Bielema, combined with the offensive wizardry and humility of Chryst, with a pinch of Alvarez managing the fates from Olympus, has given the Badgers a coaching combination unmatched in college football.

And homies, who rooted for Paul to get the head job, are happy for Heimer. Once a football vagabond, he has been able to establish a true home for his wife, Robin, and their kids, who now attend the high school where their grandmother, Patty, met their grandfather. How many big-time coaches can make that claim?

Despite the offer of big checks and jobs by the likes of Jerry Jones, Paul has set roots in home soil. Regardless of what's next, he is going to Pasadena with a team he helped create. Something he could not say as a player under Don Morton.

As for the old wall, it held on for a few extra moments. Just long enough for eight-year-old Jimmy, the youngest of the Roach clan, and his childhood buddy Heimer to head inside for a PB&J.

Moments later, with a seismic sound and shake, the wall collapsed in the exact spot where the boys had been playing. Both moms and the entire neighborhood ran outside to gawk at the wreckage, chilled by what could have happened if the boys laid beneath the bricks.

But fate intervened. Both friends are doing well these days. Brother Jim has taken it upon himself to leave voicemails for Paul during games, chiding him for passing so often at Camp Randall that he is going to give Barry agita.

The wall has been replaced. A new one stands there now. Both families have moved away from the neighborhood with only one regret.

We should have planted rose bushes.

O7.11
DIRTY LITTLE SECRET

....

But how would you feel when, upon shaking Daniel Craig's hand, you discovered that his breath was worse than Uncle Joe's?

It is summer in Madtown.

After a spring cursed with awful weather and even worse politics, any columnist with an ounce left in the brain pan would opt to pen something light, breezy, witty and relaxing for readers to enjoy during our three-week summer.

After all, we've had enough drama, haven't we?

But no. Sadly, that is not where this is going. Instead I would like to take this opportunity to make us all the slightest bit uncomfortable. It is an unpleasant job, but someone's got to do it.

I would like to broach the topic of dirty little secrets.

All families have them. Like the time Grandma was arrested after she accidentally walked out of Macy's with that scarf. Or Uncle Joe's deplorable breath. Even cities have sad, awful tales they keep under wraps. Except, of course, Madison. How could WE have a dirty little secret?

Preposterous! Here in Madison we are damn near perfect. We are regularly voted the Most Livable City in America for children, men, women, lesbians, families, iceboat sailors, dogs, cyclists and binge drinkers.

But we do have a secret. And it is dirty. And worse yet, is it not little.

Imagine our lakes Mendota, Monona, Kegonsa and Wingra were beautiful women, say, Julia Roberts, Halle Berry, Penelope Cruz and Cindy Crawford. Or, depending upon your preference, call them Daniel Craig, Denzel Washington, Matt Damon and Bradley Cooper. You have seen pictures of them. You have admired their natural, unblemished beauty from afar. They look just about perfect. And then finally one day you get to meet one of them in person. What a thrill!!! Your heart goes pit-a-pat.

But how would you feel when, upon shaking Daniel Craig's hand, you discovered that his breath was worse than Uncle Joe's? Or that Cindy

Crawford had a thin film of green scum over her teeth? Or Bradley Cooper carried a dead carp in his shirt pocket? Just how beautiful would these people seem to you then? Worse yet—what if, after shaking hands with one of these supposedly beautiful people, you immediately broke out in an itchy swimsuit rash?

And that, dear readers, is what you call a metaphor for Madison's Dirty Little Secret. Our lakes are not nearly as beautiful as they look from afar. In fact, delude all you want, but the truth is that they are deeply troubled, smelly and befouled. In the next few weeks, like December ice, they will slowly cloak themselves in a film of algae and debris none of us likes to consider or discuss. And why?

Because we are embarrassed for ourselves.

We know that it is just not right to have empty, closed beaches. We know that the only thing more shocking than a shoreline bordered by August scum and algae is that we are now used to it.

It is a reality all the more difficult for Madisonians of a certain age who remember a time when our beaches were actually open. When Madisonians waded with delight at The Willows. Cannonballed at BB Clarke. Eased our way down the sandstone steps at Tenney Park. One local writer even met his bride at Vilas Beach. If he were a young man today, such a meet might never have happened, and he would have remained a lonely, besotted bachelor forever.

All of this is even more difficult to stomach because our lakes are among the most studied bodies of water in the world. Every student who ever attended Wisconsin took Limnology 101, puttering out on Mendota on a small research craft. We have done an excellent job of graphing our lakes' demise. We know exactly what is happening — that the nutrients from our fertile agricultural lands that give us our wonderful farmers' market have become, with an awful symmetry, our lakes' worst enemies.

We know the problem and the facts. But somehow, we can't summon the will, plan and resources to save these waters. Indeed, if these elements existed, we would have no secret to hide.

So perhaps it is time for a lakes intervention. A conscious, public end to our shared self-delusion. A gang confession that our Mendota, Monona, Kegonsa and Wingra are our Dirty Little Secret. Only then can we get to a place, in a polarized political time, where we come together—government, citizens and business alike—to solve a problem we all share. The newly formed Clean Lakes Alliance could be the start we need.

And if we don't?

Well, then we'll have another Dirty Little Secret.

And that will be that we chose to do nothing at all.

10.11
BE A TEAM PLAYER

And that is actually not a problem for the citizenry. That is a problem for you.

Eric Olive is unhappy. And worried.

At least according to the *Wisconsin State Journal*.

Here is the *State Journal's* quote regarding Eric and his consternation. "Eric Olive, who lives about five blocks from the stadium on Chandler Street, said he accepts that there will be noise and additional traffic on football Saturdays, but not weeknights. He said he feared for the safety of his 8-year-old daughter because of the extra traffic ... 'I think it's rude,' Olive said. 'I think it's disruptive. I think it's unnecessary.'"

Eric is not alone. There are other people who live near Camp Randall who have voiced their concern about crowds, drunken behavior, noise and traffic. They don't like it.

Well, that is unfortunate. Obviously, no one condones rude behavior and public peeing.

But as someone who grew up in that neighborhood and worked there for two decades, let me suggest that there is another way to look in the kaleidoscope: that the people who move into the Camp Randall neighborhood, and then choose to complain about it, are one of the following ... A. Unintelligent, B. Naïve, C. Selfish or D. All of the above.

And, moreover, there is a very sane, rational and compassionate argument to be made that Camp Randall is actually an underused facility for Madisonians and Wisconsinites.

Before investigating that position, let's review why kvetching about Camp Randall could be unintelligent, naïve and selfish.

First, Camp Randall has been a stadium since 1917. Prior to that it was a military training ground and prison camp, with soldiers peeing everywhere. If you have invested in a home in that neighborhood any time in the last 150 years, unaware of the site and its attendant activities, you were not a smart buyer. In fact, it could be argued that you are dumb. And that is actually not a problem for the citizenry. That is a problem for you. And you should move. Because no one should be unhappy about where they live.

Further, if you bought in the Camp Randall neighborhood thinking you would not be affected by the nearly 80,000 visitors who swing by your house six or seven times a year, you are at least naïve. Most other adult humans know that you are bound to encounter a few asses out of 80,000 people. That is simply common sense. And if you lack common sense, you are naïve.

Also, before complaining, the few unhappy folks in the neighborhood under consideration would be wise to consider the impact of Badger football at Camp Randall in its totality, lest you be accused of selfishness.

The games bring in millions of dollars to the local economy and the coffers of one of the greatest public universities in the world. These revenues fuel research, tuition control, minority scholarships, non-income sports, small-business vitality, local charities, food suppliers, lawn parkers, T-shirt hawkers and, yes, liquor stores.

But the common benefit is more than money. The games are a celebration of community, in a neighborhood that belongs to us all, not just a few. These gatherings allow us to have fun in a way that answers a basic human need for togetherness, tribal ritual and celebration. Camp Randall games also create a national focus on our city, state and people in a unique and most times flattering way. Yes, there are excesses, but those negatives are far outweighed by the benefit to all.

So, if you have moved near Camp Randall but see only how your small life is affected, well, then, you just don't get it. And you should move.

Because there should actually be MORE events at Camp Randall, not fewer. Madisonians still talk about the concerts of U2, The Rolling Stones and Pink Floyd that were held at Camp Randall. (OK, Genesis, not so much.) These live performances were a cultural event like no other.

But the music, and the people who liked it, drew complaints from the neighbors.

So, no Simon and Garfunkel on a warm summer night. How sad that a few should deny such bliss for so many.

But back to Mr. Olive. It is a sad thing that you are upset. As a dad, I respect your concern for your daughter. The Nails' Tails sculpture alone would be cause for great paternal frenzy if my daughters were walking past it every day.

But as someone who grew up as a child on the streets of Regent and Monroe, I learned the valuable skill of adaptation, developing the skills required to cross those streets safely. And to this day I cherish the memories of the games, marching bands and the visitors from afar.

Perhaps your daughter will too, and then you will be able to see past frustration to the joy we all get from visiting your neighborhood.

11.12
FIELD OF MEMORIES

To be inside that remarkable ballpark is to go back in Madison time.

Nearly the entire family made it.

We ventured from the west side to an east side landmark that, though changed, holds memories aplenty.

My nephew was in town from college. He was roaming the turf of a beautiful, yet oddly shaped field. It is a plot of land that is as rich with moments as any single location in Madison, including Camp Randall.

Outside the traffic was whizzing past the extinct Smart Studios and new Shopbop offices on East Washington.

Just down the street the Roach clan was gathered inside Breese Stevens Field.

To be inside that remarkable ballpark is to go back in Madison time.

Breese Stevens Field was built back in the '20s. It was the first field in Madison to have lights. The façade and grandstand were added in the '30s with Depression-era funding. The rock walls came from the Hoyt Park quarry on the west side.

Even Dad, now 83, made his way into the bleachers this night. It was difficult for him. Not because he is infirm. No, the challenge for Dad was far more demanding than old age. Dad was at Breese because he had to watch his grandson play soccer.

He isn't much for soccer.

Dad quickly changed the moment from "a game where no one scores" to his most powerful memory of Breese Stevens Field.

It took place more than 65 years ago.

In the fall of 1946, the Edgewood Crusaders, under the leadership of Coach Earl Wilke, went undefeated in football. It is said, at least by those on the team, that they were a juggernaut. They had guys named McCormick, Prestagiacomo, Maglio, Devine, Heilman, Schwartz and yes, even a Roach. At the end of their regular season someone (my grandfather) had the bright idea to challenge the Chicago City Champions, Mt. Carmel, to a battle. Mt. Carmel chuckled and agreed.

Sitting in the bleachers in 2012, Dad recalled how they covered the turf of Breese Stevens Field with straw that late autumn, so it wouldn't freeze. Mt. Carmel made their way to Madison. They thumped the smaller Crusaders in a tough battle.

Later Dad played Industrial League baseball at Breese Stevens, in a high level of competition with Madison guys back from the war. He poked a home run out onto East Washington Avenue. It exited the field outside the second light tower. Back then, folks driving East Wash knew to expect the occasional baseball to rain down on them. If you hit one over the short wall in right it was only a double.

Traveling teams from the Negro Leagues played Breese. Dad seems to remember batting against a guy named Satchel Paige.

Later played baseball at Breese myself, in the Madison City Flyweight Championship Game, back when the city funded baseball for kids. Managed to break both tibia and fibula while clumsily sliding into home plate, never again to be as carefree an athlete.

Also played football there, but not as well as Timmy Healy, who in the late '60s led his Purgolders to victory over the West Regents in one of the most famous high school football games in Madison history. I was witness to Healy's winning field goal in front of a crowd that held close to ten thousand Madisonians.

In hindsight that might have been Breese Stevens' last great moment, and a chapter closed for Madison.

The city and Breese began to change. New ball fields and shopping malls grew on the outskirts of town. Shops on the square were shuttered, leaving the heart of our city to the politicians.

The University grew rapidly, overwhelming the rest of the central city.

Fans drifted away from Breese Stevens, and also from its more obscure but colorful events, such as midget car races and wrestling matches with the likes of Art "The Sailor" Thomas and Flyin' Fred Curry.

To sit in the bleachers at Breese is to hear the echoes of that smaller, more intimate, more connected Madison.

I am usually not one to wallow in the past but laughing in the bleachers at Breese that night with my family was a wistful moment.

It was cause to remember a very different time.

A very different Madison.

Shortly after we left the bleachers at Breese, it was announced that the Ace Hardware in Meadowood was closing.

Too much gunfire.

We were a town then.

We are a city now.

05.13
THE GREEN SHED

In the morning, the padlock would open, the hasp would swing free, and the day's activities would be revealed.

It was a magical, mysterious space.

The inside was dark and windowless with the musty smell of countless warm days.

It was also a welcoming place with gifts and surprises that would spill from it every day. When the city would drop them at the neighborhood parks around town in early June, you knew summer was upon us.

How could a green shed hold so much memory?

For those who grew up in Madison in the '50s and '60s, the green shed was the physical representation of a robust summer program. At select neighborhood parks the green huts, and young park attendants who managed them—clad in white T-shirts with authoritative blue piping—would make Madison a welcoming place for kids to do something, and nothing, all summer long.

For free.

On the near west side there were green sheds and attendants at Wingra, Vilas and Hoyt Park next to the reservoir.

In the morning the padlock would open, the hasp would swing free and the day's activities would be revealed. There would be washers, mill and checkerboards, tetherballs and colorful spools of plastic yarn called gimp. You would wind the stuff around an orange juice container and give it to your dad as a pencil holder. Or create a wonderful petroleum-based bracelet for Mom.

The city picnic tables would surround the staging areas and pockets of kids would swarm around throughout the day, with a kind of activity that must have mirrored the same doings of the Native Americans who first inhabited our lakeshores.

Occasionally a traveling theater company would arrive in a wagon that unfolded into a stage. They would put on a play. The stars of the production were other kids.

There were also things to do at the beaches. The high school kids played lifeguard, their noses covered in white zinc ointment. There were swimming lessons in the morning, in the clean water. You would lay out in the sand and flirt, back when the sun wasn't a menace.

On some summer evenings, in the shelters at the big parks, there would be dances.

Adding to all this activity would be the summer baseball leagues. It was a boy thing then as girls weren't encouraged or allowed to play organized sports. Hard to believe when you think about it.

The leagues were classified by age: Flyweight for the youngest kids and Midgets for the older boys. The games would be played in the mornings and afternoons, with durable rubber-coated baseballs for the sake of economy. Many of the fields were dirt, covered with a crust of aromatic oil, no doubt toxic, that was applied regularly by city crews to keep the dust down. The bats were made of a remarkable substance called wood.

On the near west side, the kids played on teams named The Shamrocks, Deerfield Butter and Heifetz Scrap. We'd ride our bikes to the games. The umpires were high school kids. The uniforms were simple brightly colored, silken T-shirts. Some might have a zipper at the collar. The day they arrived was better than Christmas. Occasionally a parent would attend a game, but it was no big deal.

The baseball year would culminate in a championship game at Breese Stevens Field, where the big boys played.

There would be basketball games on the outdoor courts. Fishing for bullheads and bluegills in the lagoons. The big Fourth of July fireworks show took place at Vilas Park, a tradition that ended when they realized it was too frightening for the zoo animals. That summer magic still seems doomed to move like a foster child in our town, searching for a home.

If there was a tipping point for Madison summers, you could point to the rise of the West Side Little League. The ball fields were on the perimeter of town with bleachers and outfield walls. We wore complete uniforms with pants. The coaches and umps and organizers were adults. You had to get in a car to go to practice and games. It cost money. Slowly, over time, Madison's neighborhood parks ceased being a magnet for kids.

They couldn't compete with the new malls on the far east and west sides.

So the parks program went away. So did the baseball leagues.

The lakes got scummy, so a lot of the beaches closed.

And the city got out of the business of kids, neighborhoods, jobs and summer.

02.14
CHEESE, SAUSAGE,
DOUBLE BLACK OLIVES

I have no doubt that he was singing about war and love and justice.

When you write a column, it is best to explore the things that matter. Love, war, justice. You know. The Big Things.

I often chide Brennan the Editor that she publishes too many stories about desserts and popular dentists. But with this issue, I applaud her without reservation, for she has chosen to feature a topic that matters totally and absolutely.

It is a subject that brings all mankind together and binds us in a unique, remarkable way. With this substance comes peace, satisfaction and joy regardless of our politics, gender or sexual preference. It is an offering that unites the disparate members of the human family in a way few things do. In its presence, the lamb will lie down with the lion, the Packers fan will smile upon the Bears fan, and Marty Beil will hug Scott Walker like a long-lost brother.

Yes, friends, I am talking about pizza.

Pizza, the magical food that delivers all the major food groups in just one bite. Vegetable, protein, fruit, grain and dairy all come warmly together in just one convenient and manageable slice to be held comfortably in the palm of your hand.

My earliest memories of pizza are vivid to me still. When I was a child in the Madison of the '50s and '60s, our town's menu was drab. The food was Midwestern, light brown, average-white-people stuff served at charming, erstwhile joints like Cuba Club and Rennebohm's. As warm and friendly as those places were, we still lived in a meatloaf, grilled cheese, mashed potato world.

For instance, I have absolutely no memory of a Chinese restaurant in Madison before the early '70s. Fried shrimp with Hoffman House sauce was viewed as an incredibly daring and rare dining experience akin to a trip to the Orient.

The only foreign fare we were exposed to came from the 'Bush, where Madison's loud and proud Italian community pushed our palates past Jell-O molds with suspended marshmallows. It was at Lombardino's Restaurant on the old University Avenue where I first experienced the wonder of pizza. The joint was owned and amiably run by Teddy and Jeanie Maglio and their family. My first pizza there forever shaped my world pizza view.

Teddy was a high school teammate of my dad's at Edgewood. In those hardscrabble days, my parents had more kids than net worth, so going out to dinner was a very big deal. Teddy, out of respect to his former teammate and pre-birth-control-pill family, always seated us at his largest table with a wonderfully gaudy lamp as a centerpiece and treated us like royalty. And it was at Teddy's recommendation that the Irish Roaches first tried pizza.

My first slice was cheese, sausage and black olives. That is what I still order to this day.

After the first glorious mouthful at Lombardino's, I embarked on a life whose chapters could be marked by pizza. First, after assessing the rave reviews from Lombardino's, my mom created her own baked white bread dough and hamburger pizza on cookie sheets. It was surprisingly good.

My first college roomies in an apartment on Willy Street were Madison Italian boys Paul Schiro and Phil Pellitteri. They introduced me to the wonder of having Gino's State Street pizza *delivered right to our door!* I ate Gino's pizza every night for a year. I regret not one slice.

Upon graduation, my career took me to Chicago, the city of broad shoulders and thick pizza. It was there that I experienced the true deep-dish layered pizza of Gino's East. And the fine thin-crust, fresh-topped offerings of Bacino's.

When I returned to Madison, I watched in rapture as Madison's pizza landscape expanded with Glass Nickel, Roman Candle, Ian's and the surprisingly good pie of Benvenuto's and the flatbread of Veranda.

I even began experimenting by hand-making my own pizza prior to Packers games with the aid of Gino's Italian Deli's starter kit of uncooked dough, mild sausage and sauce. I roll the dough, brown the sausage, add a thin layer of olive oil to the pan, along with a coating of cornmeal, three handfuls of sliced black olives and fresh mozzarella -- and presto: Papa Roach's Homemade Pizza.

But every mouthful of pizza I eat takes me back to my first slice at Lombardino's, at the big table with Ted Maglio treating us like the Medicis.

Ted would even have his mustachioed waiter from the homeland come over and sing an Italian aria to us.

I have no doubt that he was singing about war and love and justice.

And pizza.

OLD MEN AND FIRE

She stood on point for a moment, and then whirled and yelled
with moderate terror, "There's a tree on fire at your dad's!"

07.05
OLD MEN AND FIRE

Just then a DNR plane began buzzing at low altitude above us, and the whine of sirens began to call from far away.

It was one of the first warm, blustery days of spring at the lake up north.

The largemouth, like pack wolves, were moving into the shallows to gorge on the first hatch of the season. The trees, always several weeks behind their southern friends in Madison, were finally starting to bud.

It had been a dry spring in the Minocqua area. Last fall's leaves lay like a million scraps of thin parchment in the state forest that adjoins our cabin.

I was reading John Sandford's latest pulp opus, while Diane and her sister Mary were bustling about, doing little spring projects that could be seen as something or nothing at all.

Suddenly I caught a whiff of it.

"Does anyone smell smoke?" I asked.

Mary chimed right in. "Yeah. I smelled it too."

We both looked to the remains of our campfire from the night before. There was no smoke to be seen. Diane, in her careful way, had made sure to hose the smoldering remnants before we went to bed. If this had been the Roach Brothers' fishing trip, we would have put out the fire in a more primal, male fashion that several cans of beer allow men to do.

Suddenly, a wave of smoke scudded across the little bay that separates our place from my dad's cabin. "Someone must be burning something," I pronounced. Could be Dad, or the neighbor that separates us, a fellow I have not talked to in several years.

Still, there was something unsettling about the smoke. In hindsight, I think it was the quickness and volume with which it appeared. Mary, an energetic but skittish sister-in-law who the night before had mistaken a June bug for a bear, hustled down to the pier to get a better look. She stood on point for a moment, and then whirled and yelled with moderate terror, "There's a tree on fire at your dad's!"

I hurried to my car, barking to Diane, "Call 911!"

I have never driven faster on the dirt road to my folk's place. I flew down their drive and peeled onto their gorgeous lot that overlooks the lake.

My dad is a funny Irishman. He takes things pretty much in stride, as befits the solid ballplayer that he was. But the look on his face when he turned to me was genuine concern. A fire was spreading across the lawn and into the trees along the shoreline. And it was everywhere. Through the smoke I could see the neighbor beginning to work the flames with his garden hose. One large fir, thirty feet tall, had already gone up. "Looked like a blowtorch when it went," Dad yelled as I ran toward the flames. "Scared the hell out of me."

This was a fire past stomping, and Dad didn't have enough hose to reach the site, so I ran into his garage and grabbed a bucket, then dashed into the lake, shoes and all, and began to ferry water onto the blaze as it headed towards the bigger trees, the neighbor's cabin, and the Northern Highlands State Forest behind it. Just then a DNR plane began buzzing at low altitude above us, and the whine of sirens began to call from far away.

Soon, with a little hustle and adrenaline, and a helpful neighbor with enough hose, we had the thing under control.

Just then the three fire trucks arrived.

In typical fashion, Dad piped to the fire crew as they dismounted, "Well, I'm finally getting my money's worth for all those volunteer fire department raffle tickets I've been buying for twenty years!"

And so our chance to rival the conflagration at Big Flats was stopped. It turns out Dad had burned some minor trash in the campfire, waited for the flames to die, and then headed into his place for an hour nap. He was up again and watching the Cubs when he noticed the smoke and headed outside just in time to see the fir go up.

The fire had smoldered and gone latent, been given new birth when the dry afternoon winds picked up and lofted an ember some five feet from the fire circle into the pine needles, where it simmered and erupted along the shoreline. Dad received an educational brochure and explanation from the kindly DNR forestry woman, who provided us all with some thoughtful fire perspective.

Coulda happened to anyone was the general consensus, though that did not keep Dad from being embarrassed.

Later that day I ran into town and bought a bottle of Crown Royal. Went over to the neighbor I don't talk to and handed it to him. Thanked him for helping my dad. Shook his hand.

They say sometimes forest fires are a good thing. They allow a forest to be reborn. Maybe that's so. All I know is that it was quick and scary and, in a strange way, fun.

And that I shook a guy's hand that had gone unshaken for a long time.

One last thing.

Dad showed up at our cabin at seven the next morning.

He had already been to town.

In his car?

10.08
THE WORLD AND THE WOODS

....

But the trip into town can be tiresome. It is, after all, four whole miles.

Unlike a lot of trades folks in the Northwoods, Brian was right on time.

He even came out to the cabin earlier in the week to check our shot to the satellite, making sure that we had clearance over the soaring white pine on the south end of our property.

There had been much debate between the bride and me over this move.

For fifteen years our cabin was without a modern television link to the world. No cable. No dish. No static and noise. Just music, books, silence and the natural sounds that only a lake in the woods can make. You know … wind in the trees, loon calls, waves against the shore. Bliss.

The bliss that comes only when there is no television.

If there were a big game to be watched, I would make my way to the nearest tavern and nurse a beer or old fashioned. Or both.

If there was breaking news, we would turn on the radio. It could have been 1930 when the AM told us of Princess Di's demise, and the terror of Oklahoma City.

But we are in a different place in our lives now. The kids are out of the house and if we plan right, we can spend more time at the lake. Now only work requires the planning. And even that has changed.

Thanks to the growing digital dawn, we, and the rest of modern mankind, are finding that much of what needs doing can spring forth from our laptop.

Office? We don't need no stinking office!

E-mails, proposals, projects analyses and video reviews all can be handled from the green leather chair that looks out over the lake and the Mac on my ample lap.

But speed has become a factor. Because the web can now deliver so much so fast, our dial-up has become as quaint and obsolete as a rotary phone. It is simply not enough to get an e-mail any longer. You now have to lift a vast assortment of heavy digital objects.

For the last year we have adjusted by scooting into town to the WiFi coffee shop and washing down baked goods with freshly brewed coffee as we graze the web for work and news. Not uncommon for the iPhone to be retrieving one e-mail as I am sending another on the laptop while at the same time licking cinnamon from my fingers while also checking Madison.com, the NYT, CNN, Drudge, The Onion, ESPN and local radar.

But the trip into town can be tiresome. It is, after all, four whole miles.

So, I began examining the possibility of installing high-speed wireless on the lake. This required more serious marital negotiation.

There has been pressure for years to get satellite TV at the cabin. To her credit, Diane has staunchly defended the sanctity and quiet. But I argued, in my wired way, that we could enjoy the lake for more days if we at least allowed the minor intrusion of the internet.

"I mean, it's not like it's television," I pleaded.

And then I threw down the maternal instinct right bower, "And we can communicate much better with the kids!"

So, the bargain was struck.

The dish went up on the roof. Brian came inside and helped me set up the Mac. And suddenly, bingo! The world was at my lap. Fast and clean and unimaginable broad of band. Pandora will place the music genome project at our feet. Wikipedia will allow us to analyze loon calls to determine just what those two on the lake are saying about us. Radar will quickly inform us as to what is in the clouds above our pines. Will it be rain or snow?

As he was finishing up Brian informed me that the only real problem with our high-speed feed would be if ice and snow collected on the dish. He advised me to put a light treatment of oil on the pan prior to winter. I mustered up all my Northwoods manhood and asked him bacon grease would do.

Brian was cleaning the worksite when there was a honk from the drive. It was Mr. Firewood (yes, that is what he calls himself) and his dump truck loaded with oak and maple for the winter. Most days we can heat the cabin with the fieldstone fireplace alone.

He dumped the two cords of wood at the base of our new satellite dish.

Plus ça change, plus c'est la même chose.

03.10
FRIENDS ON ICE

"I am tired of being miserable. I am going to leave my wife."

It is that weekend.

For seventeen years I have hosted a gathering for my Chicago media elite friends in the frigid wasteland of northern Wisconsin. For three days we are not husbands, fathers, bosses or employees. We simply exist. As guys.

We go off the grid, and onto the ice.

The original intent of the escape was mass self-irony. Not one of us had ever been ice fishing. Standing outside in the cold trying to pull a fish through a hole was an alien act. Which is why, as men, we did it.

To indicate how unprepared the city boys were for the wilds of Vilas County, buddy Mike arrived wearing a thin Members Only jacket and loafers sans socks. In his arms he carried a large bowl of bean soup his wife had lovingly prepared for us.

It was difficult to figure which act was more troubling: going sockless in the single-digit temps or bringing a pot of beans to a male gathering.

Mike's blue feet and a post-soup cacophony akin to an Olympic fanfare were equally disturbing events.

Two of the other guys, Rino and Ron, thought they were smart. They stopped at an Army surplus store in Chicago and purchased what they presumed was warm-weather gear. They were actually Korean War HAZMAT suits with no insulating properties whatsoever.

Because we were neophytes and would become wolf bait within ten minutes if left alone on the ice, we did one smart and rare thing. We hired a guide.

George was a sweet, grizzled Vietnam vet who had hunted and fished the Northwoods since the day he returned from the jungle. He selected the lake, drilled the holes and waited for the urban dandies to drive onto the ice. Then he dropped the baits while we reclined on plastic chairs, beer in hand, hoping to spy the bobbing red flag. It was both a glorious and pathetic activity.

The trip has made for unending laughter and the occasional epiphany. One of the guys had an openly troubled marriage. On a Saturday morn he went for a walk along on the lake as the snow fell quietly. He returned to the cabin, stepped inside, shook the snow from his shoulders and declared, "I am tired of being miserable. I am going to leave my wife."

And he did.

Through the years, time and reality have intruded on our trip.

Mike was diagnosed with cancer and is successfully fighting the bastard. Varying combinations of business tensions have added drama to the trip, only to dissipate after the first beer and become comedic fodder after the second.

Unfortunately, those tensions mounted and became too toxic, to the point that we have not made the trip in two years.

Friendships ebb and flow in mysterious ways. Not all annual trips last forever.

Some friendships have a season that ends.

But this year we are trying again. Johnny, an irrepressible cat, has been the catalyst. So we head to the wilds once more, though one of our brothers has decided not to attend. A hatchet that refuses to be buried. So be it.

Friendships have a delicate chemistry. They can be memorable and outrageously funny, but the bonds shift and change.

So to the woods we traipse, knowing the constants that bind us; guys of a certain age, with similar talents and tastes. Men who have married and fathered children. Done remarkable and stupid things.

At its core, this escape was always and is still about friendship. For whatever reason over the years, we have found ourselves to be great company for three straight days. We've shared the therapy that seventy-two hours of nonstop laughter can provide. Can't say that about just any group of guys. Get the wrong crew and there will be bodies on the carpet in an hour.

As life lumbers on, I find myself wistful about friendships, particularly the older ones that have managed to endure.

Sure, these trips can be a hassle. There is food to buy, schedules to coordinate, egos to juggle.

But when you consider all the time and effort we waste on meaningless acts, surely it is worth three days to preserve a few friendships.

Even if it means standing on the ice for five hours.

07.15
EXODUS

The ritual that accompanies these summer jailbreaks is as predictable as it is entertaining.

We are now in the season of the Great Escape.

Soon millions of us will seek comfort in the beautiful woods and pristine lakes of our great state.

We long for that change of scenery, a respite from the workaday world we inhabit for eleven and a half months of the year.

As a seasoned escape artist who never misses a chance to blast north for the quiet of the woods and the soothing waters of the lake, I watch with delight as friends and family avail themselves of this luxury in the summer. This is ritual that accompanies these summer jailbreaks that is as predictable as it is entertaining. It goes something like this …

Phase One: Escape Planning. Wherein visitors ask the following questions of themselves or their hosts: Who has the sunscreen? Insect repellent? Beer? Wine? Vodka? Ice? Do I need to bring a pillow? Sheets? Towels? Are there ticks this year? What kind of ticks? Have you seen deer? Bear? Wolves? Should I bring rods? Bait? Did you say there were ticks?

Phase Two: "We're Here!" Exit car or van. Inhale deeply. Express joy at finally being here. Unload clothing and, most importantly, lug in three coolers filled with anything and everything known to man that needs cooling, from beer to baby bottles to steaks to more beer to the last cooler, which is cooling only five bags of ice and nothing else. Phase Two then proceeds with staking out sleeping quarters, a fine art that practiced hands do well by finding the darkest cubbyhole free from traffic. Then follows the first promenade down to the lake. There is another exclamation of joy, a serious examination of the waters for fish and the wonderful moment where you slip off your shoe and dip your toe in the clear waters of the lake and pronounce, "It's not that cold!"

Phase Three: Launch. In this phase, the full vacation begins. The kids change into swimwear and launch themselves into the lake with squeals of rapture. Adults sit and chat, catching up. Eventually the adults decide to swim. The majority of adults enter the water slowly, allowing themselves time to acclimate. The women are sure to issue "ick's" if the lake bottom has even the slightest bit of muck or weeds. And then that one uncle launches himself off the pier with the howl of a banshee and splashes anyone within a half mile of his dive. Happens every time.

Phase Three: Let's Eat. All food on vacation is done on the grill by the men because no self-respecting woman wants to do anything in the kitchen during a vacation. The men all fuss over the lighting of the fire, as we must have done long ago in caves after bringing home a flank of mastodon. Every single man present has an opinion about how to start the fire, if the coals are "ready" and when the burgers, chicken or brats are officially "done." Every man must at some point poke the coals. It's mandatory.

Phase Four: The Campfire. This is the best moment of the vacation. Instead of repairing to separate rooms, televisions or digital devices after dinner, the smart vacationers head down to the shore and build a campfire. It is here where the elders teach the next generation about kindling and dry wood. And then, as the summer sun sets, flames light the faces of those you love as they gaze at the moon, stars and now-still lake. The children *oooh* and *aaah* as the loons greet the rising moon. And then there is reconnection. We talk to each other. Laugh. Sing. Remember. No one but infants are put to bed. These warm summer nights are meant to be shared by all for as long as possible, for these are the moments we dream of in January.

Phase Five: Departure. Sometime during the vacation, you begin to count the days. And then it comes. Time to leave. To return to the noise and hustle. Time to once again be subjected to the constant manmade din of the city and leave behind the sounds of the natural world that soothe us. Clothing isn't packed. It's wadded up and jammed into a bag. There are hugs and kisses. A last walk down to the lake to say a final good-bye. A great friend told me that at the end of their northwoods vacation, his father would stand on the pier and shed a tear, saddened he had to bid adieu to such beauty and peace.

And then the car drives off. An hour later comes the predictable call from your guests to request that you bring home the seven things they forgot at the cabin. One is always an iPod.

And then you are home. Rested. Happy. Reconnected as a family.

There is only one thing left to do.

Check for ticks.

09.17
AS SUMMER ENDS

His musical selection? "Under the Sea" from The Little Mermaid.

Already the quality of light is changing. The longest day of the year came and went nearly three months ago. The sun is slipping lower in the sky, giving us the amber light of fall, golden hour every hour.

In another month, the particulate matter launched into the sky by millions of tractors gathering corn, oats and soybeans will give us that big, fat, amber harvest moon. (I was going to call the harvest moon "orange," but that color has fallen out of favor for many.)

But let's not let this season pass without notice. Let us bid farewell to summer.

Hardly a week goes by without seeing a story about older people near the end of their lives musing about what is important. Every one of them says to work less and spend more time with friends and family. Summer is great for that.

At our place on the lake in the woods, we've had a great summer. The ability to work remotely has meant more time on our little lake. And easier to plan visits from family and friends. Each wave of guests brings its own special flavor to the lake, be it coolers filled with food, outrageous floats shaped like swans or guitars, or, as one sweet nephew did last month, a book on the art and importance of goodness.

Each makes a special noise as he or she jumps from the pier. And more than a few have a special song they like to warble by the fire pit. Daughter Mags always sings Johnny Cash's "Folsom Prison Blues," which is even more entertaining because she can't look or sound more different from Mr. Cash. One new guest to the lake, a young Madison lawyer, was invited to sing a personal favorite by the fire. His musical selection? "Under the Sea" from "The Little Mermaid." Not kidding.

There are few things I enjoy more than sitting back from the shore in the hammock and watching friends and family laugh, sing or do pretty much nothing on a windless 80-degree day when the lake is a glass mirror of the puffy white clouds above it. I smile at their exclamations when they spy a big fish in the shallows. Or at night, when they marvel at the sounds of the woods: a chuffing buck, the strange tenor growl of a bobcat or the incomparable call of a loon. Or when they walk out on the deck at night and gaze at the timeless Milky Way, or the newer members of the firmament-satellites moving across the sky.

A realization came upon me this summer. It was a vivid cabin moment. The shore was alive with our children, uncles, aunts, nieces, nephews and friends. I sat back from the activity and just watched and listened, an act uncommon for me. It would be difficult to describe a more perfect vignette, and it came to me that these times and memories are a different kind of savings for a different kind of bank. And far more valuable, not just for me, but for everyone in the scene. We were creating shared memories that will be stored in the family cloud forever and longer. And it was all because we chose to use the most valuable of all commodities to make it happen: time.

The sugar maples start turning red, just in time for the first Packers exhibition game in August. High school sports have already started their fall practices, making it feel as if August never happened.

During the late August days, the loon parents show their two offspring how to take off from the lake with long runs across the top of the water, wings extended for lift.

On Labor Day the Minocqua locals sit in lawn chairs in front of the taverns on U.S. Highway 51 with signs that read "SEE YOU NEXT SUMMER." I have yet to do this but aspire to it.

In my mind, I have hatched a plot. Some year soon I am going to follow the 80-degree windless days south as fall and winter descend from the north. I'll make my way through southern Illinois, through Tennessee and on down to Florida.

If I must follow 80 degrees all the way to Key West, well then, so be it.

For all the cost and time, the trip will be worth it. Because for that one year I won't have to do what we in Wisconsin dread.

I won't have to say good-bye to summer.

FREE AT LAST

But as the rest of America waits for the last Boomer to croak
before throwing a big-ass party, allow me to say a
few things on behalf of my class.

10.05
WHERE THERE'S SMOKE

He works at a mushroom farm and rides an organic bicycle.

I idle into one of my favorite local taverns, to sip a beer and enjoy the novel fact that, with the new smoking ban in place, I can now breathe.

Just as my beer arrives, who should plop down next to me but my old college roommate, Bong Water Jim.

To say that Jim is lost in the sixties is an understatement. Jimbo wears sandals year-round. He has not cut his hair since the Ford administration. He works at a mushroom farm and rides an organic bicycle.

Jim is happy to see me, although it takes him ten minutes to realize I am sitting next to him.

"Man, Johnny dude, sorry, I am so into thinking on this smoking ban, man, that I didn't even see you. You gonna buy me a beer?"

I oblige, and Jim begins to go off. He has always had an interesting view on things.

"Man, I am so…I don't know…uncomfortable about this smoking ban. It's like bringing me totally down."

I ask him why.

"Well, Johnny … like, I'm torn. I'm all for healthy living … I don't eat red meat or dairy. Or white meat for that matter. I'm pretty much totally soy now. So I dig the no smoking thing because that smoke, man … hey, it's full of toxins, ya know … not to mention that when we breathe it, it has already been in someone else's lungs dude, which is like … so harsh. I mean, shouldn't the right to breathe come before the right to smoke, man?"

I tell him I agree.

I suspect Jim is just getting started, and sure enough, I am right.

"But man, I am totally down with the small business man too. I've worked in a lot of these kitchens, man, stringin' some paychecks and these bars and taverns, they're small business folks. Not some big Walmart man."

I tell Jim that Walmart do not own any bars or taverns in Madison. Yet.

"Hey man, I know. It's just a downer to think that these folks are hurtin'."

I tell Jim that I agree. Jim leans towards me, the smell of organic cheddar on his breath, despite his assertion that he doesn't eat dairy.

"So, Johnny, here's the bit man. I think I have a solution to the problem, dude."

I ask Jim what his solution is. Knowing old Bong Water, this should be good.

"Well, the way I see it, they should totally outlaw tobacco smoking in the bars."

Jim pauses a moment and then looks at me.

"But smoking dope in bars should be, like … totally legal!"

I am taken aback by Jim's novel recommendation. I offer that marijuana is illegal.

"Oh, come on Johnny! Dude, it's like less of a fine to smoke dope in a bar than it is to smoke a cigarette already! I mean, come on! Open your mind!"

I tell Jim that my mind is open, but that pot smoking is not likely to become legal in Madison taverns very soon, unless we move them all to Amsterdam.

Jim will have none of it.

"Man, think about it. First … there will be less smoke in the bars because like … no one can smoke a pack of pot! You'd fall right over! But I seen some of these old guys sit at the bar and smoke two packs of cigs in one sitting. So, like the non-smokers will be cool with this 'cause there will be less overall smoke! Plus, Johnny, pot just smells better!"

A crowd is now gathering around us. I am looking for the door. Jim cannot be stopped.

"And dude, like, no one gets in fights if they have a nice buzz, so, like, we could get rid of the entire police force, man. Think of the money we would save just on State Street at bar time, man, without all those, like, rich frat boys punchin' each other every night man! Dude, like, if they had a buzz, like they would all, like, take a nap at bar time."

I have no idea what to say to Jim right now, and even if I did, it wouldn't matter. When he gets like this, you just let him go.

"Plus, dig this … the taverns will sell so much pizza with the munchies man … like, the local bar owners will become, like, total millionaires dude!"

Some folks are now nodding. Jim has connected. I suggest to Jim that marijuana is still an illegal drug.

"Johnny, dude … you have always been so uptight. Like, all our presidents smoked pot, dude."

I tell Jim that I doubt that fact.

"Yeah, man but I read it somewhere, like Ben Franklin dug reefer."

I tell Jim that Ben Franklin was never a president.

"Oh, man … you're kidding, right?"

I tell Jim that I have to be running.

"Hey Johnny, like, can I bum a fiver?"

I oblige. Jim gives me a big bear hug as I leave.

As I step out into the warm autumn night, I hear voices and laughter from the bar.

And then Jim announces he's starting a petition.

01.06
GENERATION BRIDGE

Instead of screaming at my kids to "turn down that damned rock 'n' roll," I swap iTunes with them.

Something cool is happening.

Late this fall Di and I had a few days alone at the cabin. We were to evacuate our rustic premises when our oldest daughter Kate, a UW grad and now a working stiff in Chicago, was due to arrive with a posse of friends to spend the fall weekend in the Great Northwoods. We were sad to be leaving, but happy our daughter and her friends find the lake as welcoming and restorative as we do.

Kate and one friend arrived the evening before the other guests. We told her we would be departing early the next morning before the onslaught of the rest of the gang, so as not to cramp anyone's style. But Kate was casual about our presence. We were not shooed away, and, in fact, much to our surprise, were invited to stay another day for the festivities.

When the rest of the posse arrived, they seemed genuinely happy to see us.

That, or they were great actors. Either way, we had a fine time with the crew before we took our leave.

Now granted, it is our cabin, but the notion that some young 20-somethings would invite some 50-somethings to hang with them for a while struck me as a bit remarkable.

And this is not the first time I have observed this phenomenon. I see moms and dads at 21st birthday parties…and at the Kollege Klub for graduation celebrations that heretofore did not include a parental contingent. And everyone seems to be getting along just fine, thank you.

Further, research has indicated that the latest generation of incoming college freshmen list their parents at the top of the list of People They Most Admire.

Huh?

How did the Generation Gap become the Generation Bridge?

Here are some notions.

For the last three decades, in order to curry that all-important brand loyalty, Madison Avenue has fallen all over young consumers, thus making it far cooler to be young than to be a pipe-smoking dope shopping for a big honkin' Cadillac in those black and white '50s commercials Boomers were raised on.

Instead of aspiring to be old, everyone now aspires to be youthful.

Instead of being treated with utter condescension, youth is honored. And frankly, given the level of work they have to perform in high school and college, they deserve it.

Another reason for the Generation Bridge?

The Boomers, though self-absorbed, led a revolution against conformity. Suddenly in the '60s the notion that everyone had to cut their hair the same way, wear the same clothes, adhere faithfully to authority, get married as soon as they left college, and spit out 3.2 babies before they were thirty went right out the window. There was much societal angst, but we are now reaping the benefit of that upheaval in the form of tolerance.

Tolerance for hairstyles.

And lifestyles.

This tolerance has done away with the fundamental friction of the former generation gap.

And how does this new, bridged world manifest itself?

Instead of screaming at my kids to "turn down that damned rock 'n' roll," I swap iTunes with them. Even some hip-hop. (Though I do pass on gangsta rap.)

Son JT just learned "The Weight" by The Band on the guitar, so I can sing along with him. And one of his football buddies totally digs Journey.

Last night daughter Mags was watching "The Graduate" when I came home.

And I now share the common experience of sitting around the fire by the lake with a whole slew of Kate's friends and treating them as fellow adults, not an adolescent herd to be chaperoned. When we see each other now, we talk about the lake and how Marty and Bench wandered the great woods for twenty minutes trying to find our campfire while carrying a twelve-pack of Point beer. And how we all laughed by the fire.

And that is the greatest benefit of the generation bridge.

Our relationship with our kids and their friends is morphing from the custodial model that dominates infancy through high school into something surprising and delightful.

Friendship.

Both with our children, and their friends.

And there is one last benefit to the Generation Bridge.

We can all shop at the Gap.

03.07
FREE AT LAST

We invented the half-hour drum solo and dancing in mud.

So now that Tom Brokaw has branded the previous generation "The Greatest," what title is left for Boomers?

Are we doomed to be the Phil Bengston Generation?

(He's the guy who followed Vince Lombardi.)

At first blush it seems foolish for us to pretend that we have accomplished anything compared to the previous brood of Americans.

The overcame a Depression; we medicate ourselves to achieve the same.

They conquered Hitler, Tojo and saved the free world.

We invented the half-hour drum solo and dancing in mud.

They stoically refused to discuss their heroism.

We can't stop shouting our opinions.

Or as one *Onion* headline proclaimed: "War Heroes Give Birth to Whiniest Generation."

It is easy to rip Boomers if for no other reason than there are so many of us. America has beheld our tantrums for the span of our lives. One research firm suggested that, for as long as we are around, America will be subjected to "the social tyranny of the Baby Boom generation."

But as the rest of America waits for the last Boomer to croak before throwing a big-ass party, allow me to say a few things on behalf of my class.

First, the previous generation was blessed with the moral clarity presented by Pearl Harbor, Hitler and Auschwitz.

Their actions at Normandy and Guadalcanal took great courage.

But the decision to fight was a clear and uncluttered call.

We would have answered the same beckon.

Secondly, and most importantly, the Greatest Generation wasn't so great for everyone.

Back in that day you could still knock the wife and kids around and not go to jail.

You could tell the Mills Brothers, or any hard-working black family, that they couldn't rent a hotel room in your town.

You could beat the crap out of sissy boys with no consequences.

And you couldn't really question our government.

At least not on anything important.

Even if the government was utterly and tragically wrong.

Adherence was the rule. Even if the rules were flawed.

The Greatest Generation's finest asset during the war, conformity, seemed thickheaded in a new and different time. As a child, I had a hard time assuming things were hunky dory while watching a parade of the nation's young leaders assassinated before our eyes on black and white Sylvanias.

Hell, we even saw *assassins* assassinated while sipping Campbell's tomato soup. Just as we watched, from beneath our desks, the Cuban Missile Crisis unfold.

It was hard to think all was well when all hell was breaking loose.

So when we hit adolescence and our voices change, we sued them. Used them to question the emperor's ensemble.

We asked: Is this war a good war?

We asked: Why can't that black kid go to that school?

We asked: Why can't a woman be a doctor?

To be honest, we also asked: Are you sure this isn't oregano?

We traded crew cuts for whatever shape our hair took after going unshorn for a semester. A few girls burned bras. Most just stopped wearing them for a while. Which was great, but I digress.

What did all this mean?

What is the Boomer Legacy?

Having grown up in Madison, ground zero along with Berkeley and a few other hot spots for the Boom Experience, I believe we have bequeathed the following to future generations:

Freedom.

Not wholesale freedom from international tyranny.

But the first awakenings of true individual freedom, regardless of race, age or gender. The freedom to just be whoever the hell you want to be. Elie Wiesel mused that the Holocaust was not the death of six million people, but rather the death of one person six million times.

Well maybe a twist on that thought is the Boomer legacy.

We did not free millions at once, as the Greatest Generation did, but we began the process of freeing one person millions of times.

One black person.

One young girl or woman.

One Hispanic kid.

One gay guy.

Or gay girl.

And, yes, even white males were freed. Freed from expectations they did not embrace.

So I suggest that we be called the Freedom Generation.

We could copy the Brokaw superlative moniker and call ourselves the Free-est Generation, but that would not be correct.

Hopefully that title will fall to generations that succeed us.
We just started the ball rolling.
Peace.

03.12
WE ARE ALL ELVIS

Yes. We owned lard.

Back in the '80s, I found myself at the gates of Graceland.

It was the 10th anniversary of the passing of the Pelvis. Beside me at The King's palace were my disruptive running mates, Chicago radio legends Steve Dahl and Garry Meier. We were shooting a television show titled "Greetings From Graceland." It included a sketch of a purchase from the guardian of the gates to Elvis's poolside tomb and Jungle Room, Uncle Vester Presley.

The item we bought? *The Elvis Cookbook.*

The recipes in this book were white trash heaven. They included the makings for such delicacies as Pepsi Salad and Fried Squirrel. I laughed, but not too hard. For deep inside me, and others I know, beats the heart of a white trash epicure.

If you were in a huge family of Irish children, all born exactly eleven months apart, food was not a form of healthy nourishment but rather a nightly battle for the last potato. Though a simple hunk of starch, potatoes were the closest we had to organic food.

The Huffington Post recently ran a piece on the Five Foods to Avoid. No surprise, the first two on the list were my childhood staples. White bread. White sugar. Another on the list, fried foods, were rare in our household because we would eat the lard right out of the can before my mom could bring it to a boil.

Yes. We owned lard.

Our Elvis diet was vast and glorious. First, all entrees were sandwiches. Made from white Gardner's bread. Inside the sandwich nestled a wonderful array of ingredients. There might be butter sprinkled with sugar, or peanut butter and potato chips, or, better yet, peanut butter and bacon.

A few years ago, I endured a medical procedure and was slow to regain my appetite. Fortunately, my bride knew the way to my heart. She prepared my favorite white trash comfort lunch: peanut butter and jelly on soft white bread, which I dunked into Campbell's vegetable beef soup followed by a shot of cold, white milk.

Heaven.

The white trash liquids we consumed as children were far different from the healthy smoothies of today. First and foremost, there was Kool-Aid. And then a little later, as the space age dawned, Tang. These liquids were essentially a pound of sugar, food coloring in an orange, green, red or purple hue, and one quart of water. Often, we ate Kool-Aid crystals right out of the package and then washed them down with a gulp of agua. This left a wonderful lipstick of Red Dye #2 on our lips for days.

There was also Nestle Quik and Lik-M-Ade, powdered sugar substances that you could drizzle into any liquid, including Kool-Aid, if you cared to double down.

We also consumed mountains of Jell-O.

To this day I am not sure what Jell-O is, but the rumor was that gelatin, its primary ingredient, came from horse bones. Which was cool. Like Kool-Aid, it was another wonderful mix of sugar, food coloring and water. A popular form of presentation was the Jell-O mold. Even as a child I knew this term to be redundant, because as it moved from its liquid to solid state, Jell-O couldn't help itself. It had to become a quivering mold, regardless of the shape my mom intended.

A special delight were the items creative homemakers would suspend inside the Jell-O, pineapple chunks or miniature marshmallows being the norm. When *National Geographic* recently produced a documentary about an Ice Age hunter they named Otzi, who was released from a melting glacier after centuries of being frozen in place, it made me think of those little marshmallows trapped inside their own glacier of Jell-O. Such a fate.

Marshmallows fall into the genus of white, white trash edibles. In fact, we consumed all sorts of pure white substances: white bread, white sugar, white milk, white marshmallows, white mashed potatoes, white marshmallow fluff, white frosting, white Cool Whip and white mayo. High school science class taught us that black is all colors combined.

White, however is the absence of color — or in this case, nutrition.

White is also the color of the substance inside an Oreo. I care not what that substance is. To my mind, the Oreo cookie is beyond reproach, even to this day. I will defend unto death the right to wolf down a handful of them with cold milk.

A visit to the Facebook Town Square in prep for this column resulted in a few other unmentionables, which I will now mention: Bologna (ring). Circus peanuts (the orange, non-nut kind). Fish sticks (which are neither fish nor sticks).

But the winning recipe, due to its daring combination of white trash ingredients, was French fries dunked in Coke and vanilla ice cream.

And that sound you just heard?

The head chef at L'Etoile hitting the floor.

06.18
THE GOLF BALL

The gathered throng was far more exotic to a seventh-grader than your average Blessed Sacrament pancake breakfast.

Now that we have escaped The Worst Spring Ever, Madison is setting out to make June one of the high points of the year.

And when I write "high," I mean that literally, because our town is set to travel back in time to 1968 — a world with an abundance of hair, a scarcity of brassieres, earnest protests, endless drum solos and the sweet smell of weed wafting in the summer air.

Yes, prepare yourself for the brainchild of Ben and Judy Sidran — The Madison Reunion: A Party with a Purpose, a celebration of Madison in the '60s with those who created it.

As a townie, I had a front-row seat to history. The confluence of politics, art and culture that I witnessed taught me more than any formal education I received.

The '60s in Madison is why I am who I am.

Exactly when the 1960s started is up for debate, but in Madison, the era surely didn't begin on Jan. 1, 1960. You could argue it all started in

1963 with the Kennedy assassination or The Beatles on Ed Sullivan. Or in 1964 with the Gulf of Tonkin Resolution that gave then-President Lyndon Johnson license to expand the Vietnam War with impunity. Which he did.

But for me, the '60s arrived sometime in the early years of the decade when I biked down to Picnic Point to witness something called a "be-in," featuring a band called The Sebastian Moon Trio. The gathered throng was far more exotic to a seventh-grader than your average Blessed Sacrament pancake breakfast. Even to a 13-year-old, it was obvious that change was in the air.

And weed. Lots of weed.

That impression was enforced a year later at the Westmorland Park Fourth of July festivities, when a few earnest anti-war protesters chose to distribute literature to the neighborhood folks gathered for softball and fireworks. The suggestion that the U.S. was the bad guy in a war did not sit well with members of my dad's Glenway Liquor-sponsored team, most of whom had had a few beers and a history of military service. And they let the protesters know it. When the protesters didn't back down, a scuffle broke out. I remember being shocked at the violent reaction of my dad's friends to the anti-war argument.

And then came the 1967 Dow Riots on Bascom Hill, and the '60s in Madison began in earnest.

Otis Redding's death quickly followed. And then the State Street riots, which meant that the windows at my father's place of business, Badger Sporting Goods, would be broken. Each riot had a rhythm. The march would start, the police would attempt to disperse the crowd, the store windows would be broken, then the police would call my dad to inform him of the damage and to confirm that his shop had no guns or ammunition. Then, the following day, Dad and his workmates, eyes red from the residual tear gas, would put up plywood until the glass was replaced.

This routine went on for years.

The riots had even more drama for our family when the National Guard was called out because my uncle Pat was one of the commanding officers. Years later when talking with him, I marveled that no one was killed in the riots. Uncle Pat admitted it was a concern, and then told me that none of the frontline guardsmen had ammunition in their guns. Only a few personnel were fully armed, and they held stand-off positions. If only the Ohio Guard at Kent State had been as smart as the Wisconsin Guard.

But there was a fatality in Madison.

I was in bed at our home on Vilas Avenue in the early morning hours of Aug. 24, 1970, hoping to get some sleep before the first football scrimmage of my senior year. My coach was George Chryst, the father of the University of Wisconsin–Madison's current football coach Paul Chryst, who, coincidentally, managed to win more games last year than Wisconsin did in all its seasons from 1964 to 1969.

In that early morning at exactly 3:42 a.m., our household was awakened and shaken by a thunderous explosion that resulted in extensive damage to Sterling Hall and the death of researcher and husband Robert Fassnacht. My dad bolted upright in bed and said to my mom, "One of those SOBs blew up something on campus." He was right.

Forty-five years later, I was golfing at Odana. A guy hit a shot from another fairway that landed near me. He wandered over and I pointed out his ball. He thanked me.

That other golfer was Karleton Armstrong, one of the convicted Sterling Hall bombers.

Interestingly, his ball had a big red Wisconsin "W" on it.

If you grew up in Madison, the '60s never ends. It never will.

TURN THE PAGE

Somewhere during the advent of the cell phone, I became a gadget person. This is strange, as I can barely use a hammer.

02.03
LIKE A ROLLING STONE

Hell, the only reason I am here is because someone invented penicillin.

This is an important month in my life.

Fifty years ago, on a cold February morning, I was born. Soon, very soon, I will be a half-century old.

I hesitate to write a piece about turning 50 because it really isn't that big of a deal. I feel no different. I look the same as I did last week, when I was young and in my 40s.

In fact, I have been saying to friends that, thanks to new drugs, healthier living and occasional exercise, 50 today is what 40 was a generation ago.

How's that for denial?

But we keep track of birthdays so that we can keep track of ourselves. Fifty years on the blue ball requires some observation, especially when you write a monthly column that entails offering observations. But I balk at scratching pithy perspective on how people should live just because I have managed to compile 50 years.

Hell, the only reason I am here is because someone invented penicillin.

Sure, I could write something quaint about the fact that there were still veterans of the Civil War who were alive when I was born. Or that I remember television being novel. I could sadden you with memories of JFK's, RFK's or MLK's assassinations. Or make you smile with the excitement of the Beatles shaking their bowl cuts on Ed Sullivan.

But instead I would like to describe to you my set list.

A set list is the order of songs that a rock 'n' roll band sings at a gig. To celebrate my 50th year of life. I would like to take over the Gridiron bar, formerly the Copper Grid and the site of my first legal beer. I would hire the best local session musicians I could find, slurp one Miller Lite for courage while the audience is brought to focus as the house lights dim. With its killer groove, I would play Marvin Gaye's live version of the national anthem as sung at an NBA All-Star game in the mid-'80s. No better rendition ever.

Then I would ascend the steps to sing a few songs to celebrate the accomplishment of not dying for a half century.

Hell, if Sinatra could look back on when he was 17, so can I at 50.

First, with a blues harp and piano accompanist, I would warble the ballad version of Bruce Springsteen's "Thunder Road," beginning with those wonderful words, "The screen door slams, Mary's dress waves. Like a vision she dances across the porch as the radio plays."

From there, a build with my brother Jim, and friend and business partner, Dave Fleer, joining me on stage with their guitars as well as the rest of The Best Band 500 Bucks Can Buy. With layered harmonies and fuller instrumentation, we would play the Beatles classic "In My Life."

"There are places I remember …" Great song, good Beatles harmonies with Davey and Jim.

Then we get moving. Cue the drums. Cue the sax player. Launch into David Bowie's unforgettable "Young Americans." Tough song to do, but what a great track. Hard to memorize all those lyrics when you are young. Even harder at 50. Need female backup singers too.

Keep up the tempo with a salute to our favorite locals of years gone by with the Cheap Trick anthem, "Surrender." "Mommy's all right. Daddy's all right. They just get a little weird."

Then a Van Morrison number. Perhaps "Brown-Eyed Girl," a reminder of my wife and daughters. Or "Crazy Love." Or "Radio." Or any Van Morrison song at all with the caveat that no one can sing a Van Morrison song at all well, except for Mr. Morrison.

Then a few dedications.

First a song for my parents. Something Irish. Too early in the night for "Danny Boy." Make it "Galway Bay."

Then a song for my kids, Bob Dylan's electric version of "Forever Young." There is a great cut that he sings with Springsteen. Swing the spotlight into the crowd to find the kids with the words. "May your hand be always steady. May your feet always be swift. May you have a strong foundation as the winds of changes shift."

Then a ballad for the bride. Our latest theme song, "Harvest Moon." "I want to see you dance again … on this harvest moon."

Not sure what the closing song would be. Always fond of the harmonies of Dream Academy's "Life in a Northern Town." "In the winter of '63, it felt like the earth would freeze. With John F. Kennedy and the Beatles … take it easy on yourself."

Then I would slip off the stage. Let the real musicians take over.
Sit at a table; sip a beer in the dark.
And smile.

08.09
TURN THE PAGE

Around our house, a quiet, reading husband is a welcome animal.

Somewhere during the advent of the cell phone, I became a gadget person. This is strange, as I can barely use a hammer. But with time my fascination with new technology grew to embrace the Mac, the iPod and then the iPhone.

And now I have a new toy that is every bit as revolutionary as the aforementioned.

Yes, I have a Kindle.

For those of you who do not know the device, the Kindle is a creation of Amazon.com. It is an e-reader, meaning that it is a sleek, white tablet that instantly accesses and caches books in much the same way that an iPod manages music. With a push of a button, the world's books are at your fingertips.

No finding time to rush to Barnes and Noble. No lugging seven books on a plane. No rummaging in a library. Just a wish for a book and … poof … you have it.

Magic.

And then, once you have bought the tome in five seconds for ten bucks, you can read it. Right away, in a variety of font sizes for aging eyes or reading environments.

As glorious as the Kindle is, it has made me the target of jibes from my many literate friends who view me as a Quisling.

How could anyone be less than thrilled with the feel of a book in hand? The turn of the page! The set of the font! The jacket design! The soup stain on the page that will remain forever as a memory of when those words were read! Nothing will ever replace the book!

Well, take it from someone who loves books. They are wrong.

The Kindle is as revolutionary as Johannes Gutenberg's press. Back in Johann's time, there surely were folks who still longed for reading monk etchings on parchment as those before them preferred papyrus and those before them preferred to take a stone tablet into the bathroom. But there were some early adapters who realized right away that Johann's movable type would free them to access and read more books.

Same with the Kindle.

The effects of the Kindle on me have been profound. Always an avid reader, I now read three times as much as in my pre-Kindle days. And a greater range of books, both fiction and non-fiction.

Moreover, I am a more informed citizen. If it were not for the Kindle, I would not have read Thomas Ricks' *The Gamble* or Jane Mayer's *The Dark Side*. In fact, the very technology that has rendered the local paper nearly obsolete and left me longing for hard facts in a world of soft blogs has given me more and better information on this back side of the tech curve.

And one unintended consequence of the Kindle? My wife is happier with me. I now spend more time reading on our deck than gabbing at the rail of the Village Bar. And our television is not blaring the Brewers quite as often. Around our house, a quiet, reading husband is a welcome animal.

There will no doubt be another beneficial effect of the Kindle. In a few years, eighty-pound backpacks on the shoulders of fifty-pound scholars will go the way of walking ten miles to school in waist-deep snow.

Young students will simply have a small, nimble reading tablet with all their texts. And they will be able to reach into the ether and catch books they want to read themselves for the pure love of it, with the only impediment being a minimal cost. And as any good parent knows, a book for a child is not an expense. It is an investment, one that delivers quick returns.

That dexterity is the beauty of the Kindle and this new world.

Although I too like the turn of a printed page, words crafted into ideas are the primary appeal of books. And that benefit has not changed. The words that take us elsewhere and allow us to visit worlds we do not know still remain. The only thing that has changed is that we, the readers, now have more control.

We are now freer to access those words, without the cumbersome process and cost of printing and distribution by truck. Without someone deciding what books we can read and what books slip out of print.

Soon, as this latest revolution takes hold, no book will be out of our reach.

This past winter, I was north, alone at the cabin. I leaned back in the leather chair, with only a reading light and the fire holding off the darkness. I turned on the Kindle to read my book in progress, and a small icon in the upper right-hand corner of the device flickered at me. It told me that, even in the far reaches of the cold Wisconsin woods, I had Kindle service.

The books of the world could come to me across the night and over the snow, in an instant.

Alone, like a madman, I hollered with glee.

Magic.

01.10
HOW TO PARTY

To make a successful party, you must surround yourself with people you can insult.

With an impending New Year's Eve, it would seem unlikely to take party advice from an aging boomer. But hold on. Boomers invented parties. They were in mud, but they were fun nonetheless.

I pride myself on producing parties. Not with decorations, themes or exotic locations, but with a few tools I keep in the trunk of my car.

Before revealing The Secret Party Tools, let us define "party" by determining first what isn't a party. A party is not a collection of milling, besweatered people tangentially linked through weak social contacts guaranteed to bore you into metamorphic rock. Said rock is created by slow, grinding, unrelenting weight over endless eons.

Secondly, a party is not the swapping of trite observations concerning the following: weather, Christmas decorations, *Dancing with the Stars*, your life in Christ, Josh Groban, pet cancer, Mary Kay Cosmetics or other pyramid selling programs.

Also, a party is not a place to avoid discussions of sex, politics or religion. Indeed, it is a place where it should be fostered and encouraged, with the caveat that no one take any opinion personally and that any guest can declare your opinion as stupid without loss of friendship.

Which gets to a key party component: personnel. To make a successful party, you must surround yourself with people you can insult. It is not a party if you must be falsely polite to people you don't know for an entire evening. I am most happy when I can utter to a male attendee, "Try to pick a sweater that makes you look fatter." And he responds smoothly, "Thank you. I envy any man who needs no sweater to accomplish the same."

I also like parties where I can say to another guy, "Your wife is hot." And he thanks me and offers me his drink.

But what makes a great party?

Two things: singing and dancing. If you are at a party where there is no singing and dancing, it isn't a party. It is a get-together.

Why singing and dancing as criteria? First, it is release. You talk casually at work. But you don't sing and dance.

Secondly, singing and dancing unveil who you are more than any words you might speak. Song and dance either reveal or release inhibition. Willingness to sing and dance is also a statement: "I like you to the extent that I will be a fool before you."

But now to the crux of the affair. How do you make your guests do it?

Well, a little alcohol never hurts. But to reach critical party mass, much more than booze is needed.

First, lighting. No one, especially dorky white people, will sing or dance when the lights are full. Plus, research has shown that for each watt decreased, guests lose one year of age.

Secondly, no party ever went tribal with cheap speakers. In order to achieve orbit, guests must experience music by immersion; great music loudly played. Turning the speakers up is also a fine way to cull the party herd. The delicate and repressed will head right to the car.

Finally, there is the Party Secret. And that secret is this: the music must be right throughout the night! It must be managed. If done correctly, singing will occur. If done by a maestro, both singing and dancing will burst forth, and thus you have achieved Full Party.

In the trunk of my car lies a tool set designed as a launch mechanism for gatherings that long to become a party. In this kit is a first-rate iPod boom box, the appropriate cables, an extension cord and an eighty-gig iPod with eight thousand songs.

It is the selection of songs that will make a party sing, and in some cases, dance.

These rules quickly: Start slowly with evocative songs, strong on melody and lyrics appropriate to the age group in attendance. Play songs that trigger memories of first dates, road trips, college parties, etc. Singing should break forth spontaneously.

Read the room. When ready, add groove. This is not accomplished with white country artists. Make the first songs easy to move to. Gauge the first dancers. Give them the songs they need. Once folks dance, keep them dancing. Never clear the floor, even if "American Pie" is requested. Subtly truncate songs that aren't working. Read the room constantly, with the next song ready to go.

Finally, push the music with the best grooves to get all on the floor. As Chuck Berry once said, "You gotta make all the girls move their hips." Once that has occurred men will follow, and you will achieve Full Party.

And the greatest benefit of Full Party? It is too loud to discuss Mary Kay Cosmetics or cat tumors.

In fact, if you're lucky, you don't have to talk to anyone.

Happy New Year.

03.11
THE COOLEST PLACE IN TOWN

You cannot find a more interesting cross-section of Madison residents anywhere else in town.

I am of sufficient years to recall when it was pasture.

I am not a shopping mall creature in the same way I am not a theme park guy.

Too many people. Too much artifice. Too little quiet.

Face it: a consumer orgy is no place to read a good book.

But lately I have become a frequent flyer (not walker) of West Towne Mall, the large shopping factory with the quaint "e" at the end of its "Town." The reason for these frequent visits, however, is not about the past, but about the future. For housed in the wide corridors of West Towne is "The Coolest Place in Madison."

And I ain't talkin' Cinnabon.

I'm talking the Apple Store.

Sure, there are other cool places in town. The Union Terrace. The Harmony, Cardinal or Crystal.

But right now, at this time in the history of mankind, there is no cooler place in Madison than the Apple Store at West Towne Mall.

There is a litany for this coolness. First there is the new world dominance of Apple products: the beauty and functionality of their design, their category-defining product introductions, their unrelenting march to create a digital proletariat experience, and the business and creative genius of illness-haunted Steve Jobs.

For my money, Apple is America's twenty-first-century replacement for Standard Oil, General Motors and IBM. These blue-jeaned wizards have not just redefined the business of computers. Their creativity, modernized Yankee work ethic and ingenuity has forever altered other global businesses, including music, movies, books, telephones, academia, travel and home entertainment.

Right now, Apple is simply the best American capitalism has to offer.

And, yes, here is the compulsory nod to China and the production capabilities they offer Apple that America can no longer afford to deliver. But mass production isn't what will keep America or Madison great. Innovation, initiative and the occasional brilliance that evolves in a free society will. You can produce a touch-screen iPad anywhere in the world. But you have to be in a very special place with special people to conceive of it and bring it to market.

The Cupertino folks have also managed a stunning trick in their retail locations. Not only have they remade the gadget, they have reinvented the American shopping experience. A trip to the Apple Store gives you a pleasurable peek into what America can be.

For there, in the white environs of its Madison retail space, you travel to Planet Apple—a personalized buying trip that registers you online before your visit, checks you in, allows you to touch anything you might buy, chat with a tutor or genius, check out as you stand in the aisle, all the while surrounded by a bevy of smart, engaged, thoroughly trained folks who—get this—actually seem to care what you want.

In short, it's not Home Depot.

But the coolest thing about the Apple Store is neither the gear nor its employees.

It's the customers.

You cannot find a more interesting cross section of Madison residents anywhere else in town. There are swarms of old folks, young folks, city folks and farm folks in every skin tone imaginable, all bustling about enthusiastically from morn until night, eager to upgrade their personal entertainment, information and intellectual universe.

The most charming folks in the customer parade are the older Madisonians, those in their sixties, seventies and eighties, who are clustered throughout the store, each diving into the digital revolution with gusto. It is inspiring to see so many old open to so much new.

It is also exciting to step into the future.

Because Apple is where we can all go.

If we are smart.

If I were to wish one thing, it would be to escort government, educational and business leaders from all over Wisconsin to the Apple Store for one hour and make them watch in silence. Force them to witness the combined best of the digital new with the reassuring constants of skilled, motivated employees thrilling satisfied customers.

And in a little while they would notice something else.

Alive in employees and customers alike, there is something present that is missing in American government, public institutions, automobile, real estate, banking and other beleaguered endeavors.

It is Hope, combined with a likable touch of New American Swagger.

Which is Cool.

Which America also invented.

09.14
MY TORNADO MOMENT

"Hey, that's a hook echo. That's a tornado! And it's right by our house."

My children and bride mock me for my digital devices.

Constantly.

So do my work mates.

I would stand up for myself, but that would mean having my MacBook Air fall from my lap as I struggle to my feet entangled in the charging cords for my iPhone, iPad and iPad Mini, plus the several Jawbone Jamboxes scattered around me—which include the Big Jambox, the Regular Jambox and the Jambox Mini (which is a great little Bluetooth speaker that I put in my shirt pocket when I walk Phillip Seymour Dog and listen over 4G LTE to my "Stardust Memories" Spotify playlist, which includes over 200 different artists all singing their own version of Hoagy Carmichael's beautiful tune).

Oh. And I have three Kindles. And a Kindle Fire.

Now you may think I have a problem. Perhaps I do.

But the argument I present to those around me is that my livelihood in video production requires a keen knowledge of the many new tools that now carry the creative my associates and I produce and distribute.

Face it. Many people don't watch much TV anymore. They watch their computers, or their iPhones, iPads or some Samsung tablet or phone. So it is important for me to know how our stuff is distributed and viewed.

Frankly, I still revel in the fact that all the books, music, clothing and lawn and garden implements in the world are right at my fingertips. So is knowledge. (I Googled "Stardust" while writing this piece and in a blink confirmed the correct spelling of "Hoagy").

Here's the thing. I am old enough that the novelty of such access still amazes and delights me, unlike the young hipsters who grew up with a computer mouse in their hands … before the mouse became obsolete.

I still giggle when Siri tells me what plane is overhead in the northwoods night sky. According to Siri, that one right … over … there just left Minneapolis and is heading to London. Wow. And I remember when the only thing amongst the stars was the Sputnik.

At any rate, my digital maelstrom came to a head on the night of June 16, 2014. For that was the night I used my iPhone to monitor a tornado heading right toward my home while sitting on a couch on a small screen porch 300 miles north of the action.

Not only did my digitals allow me to watch the radar, but they also allowed me to listen to the police radios all along the storm's route from Iowa, thanks to my scanner app, which is a tremendously dorky thing to admit you have on your phone.

At any rate, on the night in question it was pretty clear that there was something big drawing a bead on our Madison home. I watched and listened to it in Minocqua as it moved from Sioux City to Cedar Falls to Platteville and then to the door of our home in the Madison/Fitchburg area. There was an exact moment when I saw the hook echo form near Platteville and said aloud to no one because the bride was asleep—and besides, she thinks I'm nuts—"Hey, that's a hook echo. That's a tornado! And it's right by our house."

And sure enough it was a tornado, right by our house. Well ahead of traditional media, Twitter and Facebook and Instagram were alive with the damage reports. One buddy posted a Facebook picture of patio furniture driven through the all of his home and into his daughter's bedroom. The scanner app lit up with a frazzled Dane County dispatcher telling everyone that Verona had been hit.

Thanks to my gizmos, I knew quickly that the tornado missed our home, but that we might have damage. And we did. When we returned home the next day, we saw that a big ash in our backyard gave up a limb to the winds.

So I went online and booked a tree trimmer.

Because there isn't a chainsaw app.

Yet.

12.17
TWENTY INCHES

I made an official notation of the first flake just after midnight by announcing it to nobody but myself.

It's the time of the year when we look to see what is swirling in the Texas Panhandle. That's the spot that spawns our big December snows.

For Madison, the most memorable of these started on Sunday, Dec. 2, 1990.

It was the best snowstorm ever.

The first hint of something big came when I had my rump in one of the sugar maples that guard the front of our house. I was doing my usual incompetent job of stringing holiday lights.

This task always included a tangle of green cords, numerous inoperative bulbs, the precarious placement of a ladder exactly 3 inches too short to accomplish the task, and several tripped ground-fault circuit interrupters. A GFCI is a device that shuts off an electric circuit if it detects electric current flowing through an unintended path, like water — or a person in a tree hanging Christmas lights.

To add to this Griswoldian scenario, I was failing at my holiday task in front of four neighbor buddies: Phil, Rich, John and Sturge. They were beneath me with Sunday beers in hand, cackling at my ineptitude. Somewhere around 3 p.m., Rich went back inside his house to grab more Miller Lites. In a flash, he trundled back out and bellowed, "Storm warning: 16-20 inches! Or MORE!"

Now, anyone who has grown up in the greater Wisconsin area is used to winter storm warnings. As the years have progressed, the warnings have become more frequent and exact. The Weather Channel will treat 4 inches of snow like the Kennedy assassination.

But even the most jaded Wisconsinite will turn his or her head when the forecast predicts 20 inches of snow. Twenty inches of snow? Damn.

The first person to react — and when I say "react," I mean it looked like he had just heard that the Japanese had attacked Pearl Harbor — was Phil. He dropped his beer on the pavement and said, "I gotta go!"

and charged into his garage. One minute later, he was speeding out of his driveway at 75 miles per hour.

The reason? Phil was one of the guys in charge of order fulfillment at Lands' End in Dodgeville back when Lands' End was really Lands' End. And the next day, Monday, Dec. 3, was the biggest day of the company's Christmas season. Phil knew he had a problem.

As he careened down the street, one of the guys said, "Hey, nice talkin' to ya, Phil."

The rest of us broke up to do the things guys do before a big snow event. Gas the blower. Find the shovels. Hunt for that bag of salt.

And then the wait began. By 5 that afternoon, all programming on our TVs had been preempted by The Weather Channel. I built a fire. And paced. Our three children were 7, 5 and 3 at the time. They thought Dad was going crazy. But I simply had Storm Brain.

The storm began innocuously. I made an official notation of the first flake just after midnight by announcing it to nobody but myself. Somewhere around 3 a.m., I dozed off. At 6 a.m., I rose and it had begun in earnest.

And for the next eight hours, the snow came down in sheets. We frolicked in the snow all day. Climbed the snow mountain created by the plows. Went sledding down the hill alongside the house.

Late in the day, all the neighborhood kids were playing in our yard. Suddenly, they stopped and stared at me from atop the mounds of snow on the perimeter of the driveway. For a moment I wondered why they were gawking. And then I found out.

Our neighbor Sturge, a former NHL hockey player, had taken a running start from his house and tore all the way down our driveway to hit me with one of the finest body checks a toothless defenseman ever made. I flew and landed in a 6-foot pile of snow. For a moment I was a big, fat snowflake myself.

Sturge and I laughed like kids. And our kids laughed like kids.

That's the beauty of a snowstorm. You can hit your neighbor and laugh.

Phil had to bring in some of his Lands' End employees via snowmobile to the office. They slept on the floor and ate Pizza Hut for two days.

By the end of that Monday, Madison had recorded its single greatest 24-hour snowfall total in history: 17.3 inches. Overall totals hit 22 inches.

So, if you are smart, this time of year you will keep your eye on that little low pressure system in North Texas.

And gas up the blower.

EDITOR'S CHOICE

It has taken thirty years, but I have learned what every man comes to understand after three decades of marriage.

"Let her have the last word."

09.05
SLOW WALTZ

Know when to shut up and walk away. And then do it.

It was a quarter of a century ago when we danced on the lawn in the late summer night.

My dad, who had never hosted one of these events, had innocently hauled out every bottle of booze he owned and simply placed them on a table in the yard. My younger brother's friends feasted on this bounty to the point where one of them, who had quaffed half a bottle of Crown Royale, dove off our front porch into the thick evergreens that bordered our home on Vilas Avenue, no doubt mistaking the shrubs for the swimming pool we did not own.

A friend of mine from Chicago presented us with a great gift: a three-hour tape of tunes with which to celebrate. It was the perfect soundtrack for the post-reception party in our yard.

Everyone danced all night.

The highlight for me was dancing with my new bride. She looked unforgettably pretty. For all the flop sweat any self-respecting groom will have, the specific act of marrying Diane was quite fun and, in a way, a relief from the vagaries of dating. I look back on my single days and realize that there was a great deal of discomforting ambiguity about romantic relationships as folks searched for their mates.

On the other hand, there is nothing ambiguous about marriage, which makes it both daunting and a relief.

This weekend Diane and I, and our three children, will head to the cabin to celebrate the twenty-fifth anniversary of that summer night so long ago. Humility aside, I consider this to be quite an achievement in these times.

Perhaps it is a sign of our success at the challenging institution of marriage that we are actually beginning to attend the weddings of our family and friends' children. At these ceremonies I sit, listen and fidget as young people and priests talk to me about love and marriage.

And it prompts a suggestion.

From here on out, no one at any marriage ceremony is allowed to talk about … define … read poems about … or offer any sort of opinion at all on love and marriage, unless someone who has been hitched for a quarter of a century or more gets to speak as well.

I think this would have a profoundly positive effect on the divorce rate.

It might also inject a bit of reality into a day full of soaring readings, grandiose promises, absolute statements and long flute songs.

And it could be pretty funny too.

It is usually obvious why people marry each other.

They can talk to each other.

They are young.

And they are irrationally hot for one another.

But the things that get you married are not always the things that keep you married.

And what are those things? Well, here are a few notions from one who has hung around in a marriage for two-and-a-half decades.

Aside from being hot for each other, you need …

The ability to negotiate.

The willingness to forget.

Humor.

The willingness to ignore.

The occasional reminder to yourself that you are not easy to be married to.

(This applies to women, too, though most often refers to men.)

You also need to …

Smile numbly and have another beer when you are overwhelmed by in-laws.

Try and keep money from being emotional. It's just a bunch of coins.

Know that sex and laughter can be practiced simultaneously.

Avoid serious relationship discussions after consuming large amounts of caffeine and/or alcohol.

Maintain constructive honesty.

Humor.

Know when to shut up and walk away. And then do it.

Apply a healthy amount of PDA (public display of affection) in front of the kids, as all children are comforted by the fact that their parents love each other.

Occasionally think about what life would be like without your mate. Humor.

Understand that mutual respect is more important than new carpeting.

Share the same page when raising kids, and then communicate it to the little darlings.

And finally, one last morsel.

When things aren't perfect, as is bound to occur, talk to someone who has been through a divorce.

I have several close friends who had the painful experience of deconstructing a marriage. To a man, unprompted, in a sad, wise tones, they have told me and the other guys at the tavern rail to avoid it if we can.

As for our twenty-fifth anniversary, my clearest memory is the dance on the lawn with my bride.

Maybe that's because marriage is just one long, slow waltz.

Sometimes on gravel.

Sometimes on thin ice.

And if you are lucky, sometimes on the soft grass of a late summer night.

Happy anniversary, dear.

09.10
SURPRISE

We had no inkling of what was to come. We were oblivious, unsuspecting.

Margaret, our middle child, came to me in the late afternoon.

Perhaps I should have seen it coming then, but she betrayed no artifice.

"Dad," she said, "Mom needs a wine cruise. This activity is too much for her." This was not a request. It was a directive.

Truth is, things were a little crazy.

Our three children and twenty of their closest friends had joined us for the annual Fourth at the Lake. The youngsters are in fact adults, recent college grads turned working stiffs. This makes the weekend both jailbreak and marathon. Many of the kids are Badger alums, and thus magna cum social. The weekend is a nonstop parade of beer pong, singing, guitar playing, short-attention-span iPoding, charades, fishing, bonfires and an hour of sleeping in any spot where they happen to stop moving when the sun comes up.

This year was marked by a beard-growing contest among the young men who then competed in shaving said facial scruff into the worst possible biker, porn star, Civil War vet, state trooper moustaches. One fellow also shaved the initials of Roach Lake into his chest hair, nearly losing a nipple while doing so. And he was sober.

It is all a wonderful social madness. But it is difficult for the bride. Like all moms, Di is prone to worry. For three days her maternal instinct is multiplied by a factor of seven as she transforms from the mother of three to mom of twenty-three ... count 'em ... twenty-three young adults who spend the entire trip acting like the adolescents we remember them as.

The festivities honoring our nation's birth culminate on Independence Day. A half barrel of Miller Lite is ferried to the middle of our little pond in a fishing boat and then hoisted to a crudely constructed Celebration Island that is, in actuality, an aging swim raft lashed to the fishing boat with cheap rope. A boom box fuels a spasm of patriotism in the form of swimsuit-clad men and women mouthing lyrics to "Motown Philly" while reproducing an inexact version of the steps once executed by Boyz II Men and then falling into the water.

Our lake neighbors sit on the shoreline in lawn chairs with their mouths hanging open in amazement as a daylong tribal dance ensues. They talk about it all winter.

All in attendance will sometime find themselves in the lake. This is funny and expected, except to Diane who polices the area in her kayak making sure that none of these little darlings drown in the nine feet of crystal clear water.

"What if they hit their head? What if they hit the bottom?" Diane will worry.

"Yeah. And what if they spill their margarita?" one of the kids will respond.

And so, it was in the wake of such activity that Maggie's mandate came. As we hopped aboard our trolling motor pontoon she announced that she would drive. "You fish, Dad."

We tooled slowly, quietly around the lake. The party had stopped. The waters were still, the evening perfect. I casted while the bride practiced deep breathing and slow chardonnay sips.

We had no inkling of what was to come. We were oblivious, unsuspecting. But why would we be leery? We were wed in August, not July.

As we came 'round the bay to my parents' cabin, just down shore from our place, the surprise was sprung. They had staged it right beneath our noses. A large banner read "Happy 30th," and there were all our young guests, now clad in makeshift polyester prom outfits and horrid blouses meant to honor the petroleum-based clothing of 1980. They applauded as we stepped ashore.

The tune "Ease on Down the Road," which we danced to on our wedding day in Gerri DiMaggio's jazzy style, wafted out into the summer evening. In honor of Diane's strange obsession with small, green amphibians, a wedding cake depicting two frogs on a lily pad was presented to us.

We posed for a group photo. The aging groom grabbed some ferns from along the shoreline for the bride's bouquet. The picture was snapped. He toasted his bride.

Then Diane spoke, "If we could have known thirty years ago that we would be with all of you today, well, it's … this is … perfect." She then began to tear up. The girls sighed. The boys went for another cup of beer.

As for me, I said nothing more.

It has taken thirty years, but I have learned what every man comes to understand after three decades of marriage.

Let her have the last word.

04.11
WORLD WAR WISCONSIN

Because this ain't no disco. This ain't no foolin' around.

Behind me Madison is burning.

It has been only a few days since the fighting ceased. Walker still holds the Capitol, though barely. Meanwhile the rebel union forces have established a shadow government headquartered in the space formerly occupied by A Room of One's Own.

Mark Miller has been named Titular Rebel Governor even though the last time anyone saw him he was wandering a mall in Tinley Park searching for comfortable shoes and clean briefs. Fred Risser has been named Ambassador to the Court of King James and will be leaving as soon as he locates his reading glasses and the pill box that has all his meds laid out for the week.

None of the Democratic senators have returned to the smoking ruins of Madison, understandable given the threats made by the Least Likeable Irishmen in Wisconsin History: the Fitzgerald Brothers. Their bullying has included arrest, milk-boarding and public stoning. Their fist-shaking has been uniformly ineffective due to their constant look of confusion, and because they named Dad head of the State Police, which isn't done even in Haiti.

The teachers have hunkered down in their papier mâché bunkers surrounding the Capitol grounds and promise not to leave until summer vacation, as they all have plans. Many of them will take a few days off from comparing themselves to black Mississippi sharecroppers because they have accumulated tons of sick days while being on strike. And their working-class brethren wipe tables at the bistro after their lunch and work 12 months a year with no health care, pensions or paid holidays.

The firemen continue to parade around the Square in support of their union brothers and sisters, their necks strained from holding up those ridiculously large helmets and borrowed equity from the NYFD. The police are confused because they guard the Capitol from the unions to which they belong. Many hope the National Guard is called out, but that is a problem because some belong to the Guard as well. Most cops would prefer to don the Army uniform. It is far sexier to look like a war hero with a big rifle than someone who has just pulled you over for 58 in a 45.

The Republican senators parade ceaselessly before the Fox News cameras with a seemingly endless array of bad suits. It is difficult to determine if their constant look of frustration stems from the absence of their renegade counterparts, or jealousy of the shopping and better haircuts available along the Miracle Mile.

Down in Chicago, Jesse Jackson is on call to stand by the protesters who love him even though he threatened to castrate the first black man ever elected President of the United States, which is at least as bad as anything said in the moronic call Walker had with an impersonator.

In the Capitol, formerly occupied by a large crowd of college grad martyrs who would have us believe they were almost killed in the Triangle Shirtwaist Factory fire, custodians are spending big dollars—that we reportedly don't have—to remove the mess left from the signs that didn't do much except promote a slumber party.

Deep within the bowels of the Capitol, where it all started, Scooter Walker plots. He is determined to prove that he is tough and ignorant. He has been reading histories of Lincoln and Churchill to find out what countries they were from. Plus, some of the books have cool pictures. He knows that times like these require leaders who can pull people apart and make them scream at each other, especially if they are neighbors, relatives or Facebook friends. He knows there will be a special place in history for him, and if he ever gets the chance he is going to take a class to learn more about it.

Meanwhile, we huddle in our basements, wondering what is to become of our formerly prosperous and friendly state that is, depending on who you ask, completely broke or doing just fine. We stack the boxes of soup and saltines we picked up at Sam's, just in case, and we worry about the pensions we do not have. The job security we don't possess. The tax bills we pay. And the politicians we elected who can't do squat.

And in an exclusive club in Manhattan, a bond trader is getting a manicure before heading over to see his mistress. When he sees yet another Wisconsin headline in the NYT, he chuckles and mumbles, "Suckers."

We can only hope that no one has a van loaded with weapons. That someone sends lawyers, guns and money. Because this ain't no disco. This ain't no foolin' around.

Perhaps someone will emerge as a real leader. Until then, the shouting continues.

From Madison, Wisconsin, I'm wearing a trench coat and trying to look as if I understand what is happening, when in fact, I don't.

Back to the studio.

09.09
BEERS AND FREEDOM

The rail was near empty, save for two guys huddled at the far end of the bar.

It was twilight, those few moments when it is neither day nor night. Passed the cemeteries on Mineral Point, turned left at Glenway. The parking lot at the Village Bar looked lonely, so I pulled in for the simple pleasure of a cold beer at the end of the day.

The lights were dimmed. The rail was near empty, save for two guys huddled at the far end of the bar. One was tall, wearing sad eyes and an Amish beard. The other man carried a quiet dignity in his white shirt and dark suit. The tall fella was white. The guy in the suit was black. Sat down next to them and nodded. "Hi. I'm John."

The tall guy smiled, "I'm Abe. This is my friend, Martin." Martin nodded and took a sip of his beer. Abe continued, "We're just visiting Madison."

Martin spoke up. "Abe tries to visit Wisconsin once a year because of the Iron Brigade." I must have looked confused. Abe looked up slowly from his beer, as if it were a struggle, and held my eye. "The Iron Brigade lost a greater portion of men than any Union force. Mostly Wisconsin farm boys." Abe's sadness was palpable.

"Such sacrifice," Martin sighed. "I honor Wisconsin for Andrew Goodman." Martin took a sip and continued. "He attended your university briefly. He was murdered in Mississippi." We all went quiet for a moment.

"I'm from Illinois." Abe brightened up. "They used to call us 'Flatlanders' up here."

I chuckled and took a sip. Not being shy to talk race, sex or religion, I asked the two if they had heard about the brouhaha concerning Henry Gates and the Cambridge cop.

Martin smiled. "We've been out of contact a while." They shared a laugh. Abe turned to me. "Tell us about it, friend."

"Well ..." I began, "a white policeman responds to a call of a burglary at an older black guy's house. Turns out that this older guy is at Harvard ..."

"A Negro student at Harvard. Well, fancy that!" smiled Abe. I turned to the gaunt guy. "He's no student, Abe. He's a professor." Martin slapped his hand on the bar in delight. "Perfect!" he exclaimed.

I took a swig. "The officer asked for identification from the professor. Then, according to some reports, the professor called the cop a racist, and the cop got mad."

"The policeman got mad, eh?" Abe said.

"He was Irish," I explained. Both nodded knowingly.

"Interesting." Martin turned to me, elbow on the bar. "The cop got mad because he was called a racist? Was a time they bragged about being racist."

I told them that the other cops, one black and one Hispanic, both sided with the white officer's account. "A black AND a Mexican policeman?"

Abe was astounded. "Are you telling me that Mexico is now part of the Union?"

"Kind of," I replied.

I described the arrest of Professor Gates, and the national controversy it triggered.

"Well, sir, I used to be a lawyer. It's a bold thing for the state to arrest a man in his own home," said Abe. "On the other hand, was a time if a Negro yelled at a white policeman, there would be a beating. Or worse."

Martin winced and chimed in. "It's no crime for a colored man to be angry, and good reason. But there is comfort that he wasn't lynched for whistling, like Emmett Till." Abe nodded in agreement. Martin paused to sip his beer, then mused, "Got my doctorate in Boston. Harvard professors can be insufferable."

Martin eyed me. "I assume the authorities sided with the white police."

"Not completely." I paused a moment. "The uh … mayor of Cambridge and the governor of Massachusetts … are black."

Martin looked surprised. Abe laughed and slapped him on the back. "Well, how about that, Martin!"

I played with the condensation on the glass. "Even the president weighed in. Invited the professor and officer to the White House to share a beer with him and the VP. You know, to find some common ground."

Martin looked up. "When I was a young man, they would not let Marian Anderson sing at Constitution Hall. And now we're visiting on the White House lawn. Wonderful."

I agreed. "Yup. There they were. Two black men and two white men, sharing a beer, just trying to work things out."

There was silence for a moment. Then Abe spoke. "Friend." He put his large hand on my arm. "You said two black men and two white men. Are you telling me we have a Negro vice president?"

I turned to Abe. "No sir, the vice president is white." I took a sip and let the statement hang.

Abe and Martin looked at each other in slow realization. Then a tear formed in Abe's eye. Martin offered Abe his kerchief, and turned to me,

"The president of the United States is a black man?"

"Yes, Martin, he is." Martin's eyes welled too.

There was silence. Then Abe spoke. "Gentlemen, a toast!" He cleared his throat. Martin joshed, "Keep it short, Abraham." Abe smiled, "Look who's talking."

Abe took his glass and pronounced, "As a great man once said, 'Let freedom ring!' "

Martin laughed and nodded, "And as another great man said, 'To a new birth of freedom!' "

Abe and Martin laughed as they threw their arms around each other's shoulders and lifted their beers.

I raised my glass with them.

07.16
ONE-CLICK JUNKIE

The fact that you can't remember what you ordered makes the deliveries all the more exciting.

It has become a joke in the office. Each day the FedEx or UPS driver arrives and leaves a package or two for me. Not every day. But many.

These deliveries are evidence of addiction.

Several years ago, I joined Amazon and shortly thereafter discovered its most habit-forming function: 1-Click.

If you are impatient, require instant gratification and loathe shopping malls, this is what you have been waiting for all your life. With a couple of presets and a credit card number, the inventory of the world awaits you.

Need shoes? Licorice? A fire starter as seen on "Naked and Afraid?" It is but one search and click away. And because it's billed to your credit card so seamlessly, it's as if you never spent money at all.

And then, like some sort of 24/7/365 Santa, your stuff arrives.

The fact that you can't remember what you ordered makes the deliveries all the more exciting. It might be socks, a big-ass flashlight, golf pants, a new cord for some appliance, walleye tiki lights or a cable organizer. The possibilities are endless.

And lest this looks like wanton spending, the price of most items ordered is less than 30 bucks. Like a thing called Drop Stop that keeps your phone and keys from falling under the car seat — 20 bucks. A pack of plastic thingies that unclogs drains — 9 bucks. A Shiatsu deep-kneading lower-back massage pillow for the outrageous price of 30 bucks. A sheet of magic polymer that protects iPad glass — 8 bucks.

The fact that many of these devices actually solve a problem makes you even giddier.

And the pure obscurity of the products is dazzling. You can find things on Amazon that no self-respecting store would ever stock because the likelihood of someone actually buying it is infinitely remote. Plus, Amazon has an incredible array of replacement parts for dopey consumers who break and misplace things constantly, which would be me.

If you click enough you become an excellent site navigator, translator of user reviews and an obsessive package tracker. "Oh look, my package has been shipped from Korea. Now it's in Memphis. Look! It's arrived locally."

It's all quite pathetic.

Another wondrous aspect of 1-Click? Like the woman who sends herself flowers at the office, the 1-Click package arrivals don't feel like you ordered them. They feel as if someone sent you a gift, even though that someone is yourself.

Pretty pathetic.

My 1-Click addiction reached another level recently when I figured out that Amazon would deliver to our shack in the northwoods. No surprise that Amazon has seen a rise in orders of mosquito netting, wood splitting tools and even more walleye tiki lights.

Of course, there can be mistakes. I ordered two pairs of John Lennon sunglasses only to receive 24 pairs. It seems I overlooked the fact that each order was actually a dozen sunglasses, so if you need some John Lennon sunglasses, I'm your guy.

Amazon is ruthless in sating my addiction. It nudges you incessantly with recommendations based on what you have already purchased. Currently, it suggests I buy a tow strap, bicycle pants, a harmonica in the key of A and a Bear Grylls Field Sharpener. Whatever that is.

But here is the 1-Click benefit I enjoy most: you don't have to interact with a single human being throughout the entire process. No salespeople. No spatially unaware people standing in the middle of the aisle while you are trying to pass. No swiping your old credit card nine times before it works. No half-hour looking for parking. No lugging packages while you sweat under your jacket. No bumping into someone you'd rather not see. And no explaining why you have 10 strands of walleye tiki lights.

Just a couch. A computer. And yourself.

Then in a day or two, the Amazon Fairy appears at your door and your wish is granted.

Of course, there is no guarantee that you will be happy with each purchase.

At least until they create a "Happiness" button.

ABOUT THE AUTHOR

2018 marks John Roach's 25th anniversary as the "back-page" columnist for *Madison Magazine*. In 2003, a selection of the first 10 years of his columns were compiled into a book, "Way Out Here in the Middle." The latest book, "While I Have Your Attention," highlights John's favorites and most memorable from 2003-2018.

He is founder and president of John Roach Projects, a video and film production company based in Madison, Wisconsin. Before returning home to put down roots and raise his family, John was a producer at CBS and ABC in Chicago for six years. He developed and produced "The SportsWriters on TV," which ran for 13 years and was hailed by *Sports Illustrated* as the template for all television sports talk shows. His credits also include six Chicago Emmys, a National Iris Award for Best Television Special and a national CableACE nomination.

John and Mary Sweeney co-wrote the screenplay for, "The Straight Story," a movie directed by David Lynch and starring Richard Farnsworth, who received an Academy Award nomination for Best Actor. The screenplay was nominated for an Independent Spirit Award. "Like Hemingway's dialogue," wrote Roger Ebert, "the screenplay by John Roach and Mary Sweeney finds poetry and truth in the exact choice of the right everyday words."

In 2018, Roach was awarded lifetime membership to the Writers Guild of America.

John lives in Madison with his bride, Diane, with whom he launched three amazing children into the world: Kate, Maggie and JT.